Women and Stepfamilies

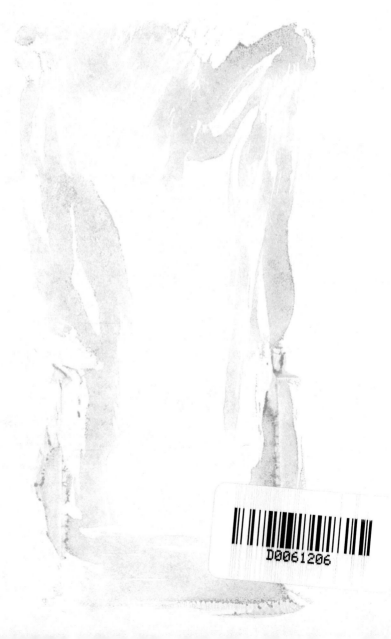

In the series WOMEN IN THE POLITICAL ECONOMY,
edited by Ronnie J. Steinberg

Women and Stepfamilies

Voices of Anger and Love

Edited by
Nan Bauer Maglin and
Nancy Schniedewind

Temple University Press
Philadelphia

Temple University Press, Philadelphia 19122
Copyright © 1989 by Nan Bauer Maglin and Nancy Schniedewind
All rights reserved
Published 1989
Printed in the United States of America

The paper used in this publication meets the minimum
requirements of American National Standard for Information
Sciences—Permanence of Paper for Printed Library Materials,
ANSI Z39.48-1984

Library of Congress
Library of Congress Cataloging-in-Publication Data

Women and stepfamilies : voices of anger and love / edited by Nan
    Bauer Maglin and Nancy Schniedewind.
        p. cm. — (Women in the political economy)
    Bibliography: p.
    Includes index.
    ISBN 0-87722-586-9 (alk. paper)
    1. Stepfamilies—United States—Case studies.   2. Stepmothers—
United States—Case studies.   3. Intergenerational relations—
United States—Case studies.   I. Maglin, Nan Bauer.
II. Schniedewind, Nancy, 1947–   . III. Series.
HQ759.92.W66 1989
306.8'7—dc19   88-11719
                                                                CIP

Contents

Contents

Contents

Preface

Women and Stepfamilies: Voices of Anger and Love began with our own personal experiences. After several years of gathering, it has grown from our two stories to many women's stories. We start by sharing our own stepfamily "tales."

NAN: I have been in a stepfamily now for six years. My daughter from my previous marriage was adopted from Colombia; she is now ten years old. My stepdaughters, Heather and Seana, twenty-three and twenty-four, are the biological children of my husband, Chris, and his ex-wife; they both are in school in New Jersey. My stepson, Joshua (sixteen), who is black, was adopted by Chris and his ex-wife when he was a month old. He lives in New Jersey with his mother, stepfather, and half-sister; my two step-daughters are there much of the time. Chris and I live in Brooklyn in a brownstone. I share custody of my daughter with my ex-husband, who lives upstairs in the brownstone. My daughter alternates days and nights, upstairs and downstairs. Chris drives to New Jersey in the middle of the week and twice on the weekends to see Josh, more frequently when Josh's basketball or baseball team has a game. Chris and I are both full-time academics.

One obvious problem for my stepfamily is time: how to apportion it, how to find enough of it for all the various segments of this two-state family configuration, and how to steal some for anything else. Another problem is money: there are many pressing needs and not all can be satisfied. One of the obvious pluses, given the variety in my extended family, is the richness in backgrounds and interests of its members. Joining my New York–urban-Jewish-radical milieu with Chris's working-class-Kansan-Louisianan-WASP past, and both with the upper-middle-class urban-suburban intellectual ambience of our current families, has led to tensions and adjustments, but also to growth on everyone's part. Such diversity seems to be common to many stepfamilies. So also must be the difficult road of accepting that diversity.

Particularly troubling for me in the beginning years of our stepfamily was the image of the "good mother" and the stereotype of the "wicked stepmother." This concern hit me most sharply in 1984 when we moved to New Jersey so that Chris could have a year near his children. The move brought up a lot of fears and anxiety in me. We would be a few blocks away from his ex-wife, *their mother*. We were moving to the suburbs where, at least in my memory and fantasies, mothers were *mothers* in the typical white, middle-class, nuclear-family way. I had waited to become a mother until, after years in the feminist movement, I had sufficiently come to terms with that institution so that I could approach it somewhat freer of its traditional constraints—working full time, not cooking much, sharing parenting and household chores, retaining my closeness to my women's group and women friends, remaining political. But when (at age 40) I joined my family with Chris's family I felt the presence of a "real" mother hovering over my life. I felt I had to compete with this presence—even though no one asked it of me. Certainly not Chris, who after five years as a single father, had redefined his earlier, more traditional ideas about marriages. Not his daughters; they were grown and didn't need my mothering (they never requested, for example, that I bake an apple pie). Nevertheless I believed that the children expected this traditional role and therefore saw me not as Nan but as inadequate mother (and inadequate wife to their father). I responded by overreacting in various ways: by refusing to wife or mother at all, being silent, or being aggressively militant about who I was. Trying to remain free of the "perfect mother" image, I inadvertently moved dangerously close to the "wicked stepmother."

Fortunately for us all, our personal histories also held the possibilities of some positive adjustments. For instance, Chris and I did not fall into traditional roles, partly because I had abdicated the traditional female one and partly because as a single father he had tried to become more of an active parent than he had been in his marriage. We also learned from each other very different and complementary styles of parenting and stepparenting; while I began to provide a more structured and scheduled pattern to the non-custodial parent-child relationship Chris and his children struggled with, he provided a warmth and immediacy of "mothering" for my daughter.

Style, of course, is not the answer to everything. Money remains an issue for us, as it does for most stepfamilies. And I continue to wrestle with the question of what it means to be a feminist stepmother to a teenage boy. However, what I see for my stepfamily is that our mixing, if not our "perfect blending," has created alternative images of relationships and roles that were not there in our previous families.

NANCY: Once, when my four-year-old son Jesse and I were having dinner together, he looked up at me with a serious expression and asked, "Are you Noelle's mother?" I explained to him that Noelle had another mother and I was her stepmother. His big blue eyes opened wide and, looking at me with an expression of utter incredulity, he exclaimed, "*You're* the evil stepmother?!"

His ongoing experience of my love was suddenly negated by the cultural power of that word. The fact that my child, who in his four short years of life had never been read the classic fairytales at home, already "knew" about stepmothers, brought home to me even greater appreciation of my struggle for personhood in a stepfamily.

My experience as a stepmother has essentially been enriching. Both my stepchildren—Dave, twenty-two, and Noelle, nineteen—and their father, Dave, are grounded, caring, and spirited people. In our fifteen years together, I have fond memories of many joyful times, from adventuring on camping trips to enjoying creatively conceived meals. I have appreciated their contributions to the varied endeavors of our lives, from household job sharing to valuable ideas and artwork that are part of my books. I have taken pride in their many accomplishments, from Noelle's blue ribbon at the county fair horse show to Dave's sensitivity and patience while tutoring a fourth-grade peer.

My experience as a stepmother has also been marked by pain, resentment, alienation, and confusion. Some of these feelings were generated by the contradictions between my feminism and the realities of living in a stepfamily. One of my goals as a feminist has been the equitable sharing of power and responsibility in institutions and relationships. In my stepfamily, decisions were often made about my life over which I had little power, yet I had to live with the consequences. For example, on several occasions a phone call from Dave's former wife would bring in its wake the unexpected arrival, for the next six months to a year, of two children and a dog into living spaces designed for two people. With their presence came responsibility but little power, a dynamic that debilitates in any situation.

I felt hurt and angered by what seemed such ongoing accommodations to the needs of stepchildren, even though they lived with us part-time. I often felt boxed in, both physically and psychological. Consequently I sometimes distanced myself from my stepchildren in order to help salvage a vestige of personal power. Although I sought family as a place of both autonomy and community, sometimes alienation set in: being "in" meant losing my sense of self, but being "out" meant separation from others.

Becoming a stepmother as a young, energetic woman, I sensed early on the importance of retaining my selfhood by "stepping out." When I did "step out," I experienced considerable guilt and confusion at the time. In retrospect I understand that my feminism, commitment to work, and independent personality helped me set boundaries on my mothering. I maintained parenting and nonparenting parts of myself, although those parts were far from integrated.

In our family I saw the physical and psychological division of labor shift from that in a traditional family. The shift was made possible, in part, because of our commitment to nonsexist ideas and the flexible schedules that we had as academics. Dave took on many practical family responsibilities, such as notes to the teacher, new shoes, and arrangements for day camp. He also took on the bulk of the responsibility for responding to the children's emotional needs. I was the backup parent and, at the same time, a significant female adult role model and caregiver. Now, mother to our own five-year-old child, experiencing the enormous practical and psychological responsibilities of full-time parenting, I appreciate that arrangement in our stepfamily even more.

Although I write some of this as a retrospective (my stepchildren are in college and no longer living with us), I still experience the bonds of living in a stepfamily. Because Dave has always had financial commitments to his children, and still is encumbered with college costs, he has contributed less to our living costs. I have often given more to our shared expenses, something I resent. The pain of the bonds of my stepfamily go deeper than money, however. I have wanted to have more than one child. Largely because of the time, energy, financial commitment, and ongoing responsibility that Dave has expended over the years for Dave and Noelle, he is unwilling to consider a second child of our own. For me this painful price of living in a stepfamily is ever present.

When I reminisce on my years as a stepmother, I tend to focus on some of our worst moments and hardest times. An experience I share with other stepmothers is that of never having been thanked for what we have given as stepmothers, particularly by our stepchildren's biological mothers. While feelings of affection and care that exude appreciation are part of my relationship with Dave, Noelle, and Dave Jr., I have seldom heard them clearly articulate appreciation of my stepmothering. Yet when I talked with them individually, as part of the process of writing this book, each offered surprisingly affirmative feedback and focused on positive experiences. To what extent, I wonder, have stepmothers' internalized feelings of "badness" set us up to filter out that which is good?

Having little contact with other women in stepfamilies when my stepchildren were younger, I often felt confused and alone. Slowly I began to understand that re-created families could be places of new forms of connectedness and love. Now that I am part of a broader network of women in stepfamilies, my alienation has lessened. I see now that the way in which we redefined our family, basically with healthy and happy results, has happened for many other stepfamilies as well. My hope for the transforming power of women's experiences in stepfamilies has been strengthened by knowledge of our collective lives.

We are grateful to each other and all the women in the book who have chosen to share their lives here. We want to thank all the many people who helped in the process of putting this collection together, especially Marti Bombyk, and also Quintana, Joshua, Heather, Seana, Chris, Jesse, Noelle, Dave Jr., and Dave.

October 29, 1987

Introduction

We, the editors and writers of *Women and Stepfamilies,* are all women in stepfamilies or women who have children in stepfamilies. We reflect some of the many experiences of millions of other women like ourselves.[1] This anthology gives voice to the anger and pain, the struggles, the pleasures, and the visions that emerge from our daily lives. We express ourselves in many ways: letters, journals, poems, stories, personal narratives, interviews, and analytic essays. Despite our numbers, this is the first book to focus on the unique and varied experiences and perspectives of women in stepfamilies as told by the women themselves.[2]

Listen to the women in Part I, Perspectives, and you are listening in on something very similar to the first stages in the consciousness-raising process that began with the reemergence of the women's movement in the 1970s. We tell *our* stories, putting ourselves at their center. Read the selections in Part II, Stepping Out, and Part III, Transforming—Both Within and Without, and you are participating in a process similar to the latter stages of consciousness raising: women look at what we have in common as well as our differences; we take our personal stories and understand them in a social context from a variety of feminist perspectives. The pieces you will read are necessarily detailed and complicated, mirroring the complexity of stepfamily life. We use the term *stepfamily* rather than *blended family* because *blended family* assumes integration and hides difference. Rather than blended away, those differences should be acknowledged and respected.

Although there have been many feminist analyses of women and the family,[3] *Women and Stepfamilies* adds a new dimension. It looks at women, their partners, and children in second, non-nuclear, nonbiological families. This is particularly important in light of the fact that, as Judith Grant points out, the traditional family (biological father, biological mother, and children) is for many people now a myth. The 1980s, however, have seen the reevocation of the image of that traditional family and an emphasis on biological motherhood. With the increasing privatization of the family in the 1980s, stepfamilies have not undergone the kind of scrutiny that was true of family life in the late 1960s and 1970s. Because of this, women and children particularly have suffered as they wrestled all alone with myths of family and problems they felt were somehow of their own making. This book allows us to rediscover that the personal is political; that our stepfamily problems are not private ones nor are the solutions totally individual ones.

Stepfamilies are no longer totally unrecognized—at least in everyday life—although they are still invisible in legislation, social services policy, and public institutions. In the last few years the publishing industry and the media have represented them; there are support groups nationwide; it is possible to buy greeting cards for several varieties of steppersons. In many cases, however, negative associations still adhere to stepfamilies, especially stepmothers. Three contemporary examples will suffice:

1. *The Charmings,* a TV series aired in the spring of 1987, updated the Snow White story to a 1980s American suburb, keeping the wicked stepmother. Snow to her husband Eric: "I can't live in the same house with her." Eric: "She's your stepmother." Snow: "She's a witch." Eric: "Yes, but she's family."

2. Dr. Elizabeth Stern (of the Baby M case,[4]) emphatically rejected the name and role of stepmother: "I do not want to be known as a stepmother. I want to be a legal mother" (*New York Times,* March 16, 1987).

3. Feminist rewritings of fairytales, while they write the daughter/stepdaughter as an active self-creator rather than a passive victim, often retain the despised and evil stepmother; see some of the tales in Zipes's 1986 collection *Don't Bet on the Prince: Contemporary Feminist Fairy Tales in North America and England.*

From the many narratives in *Women and Stepfamilies,* a revised and enlarged picture of women and stepfamilies should emerge for all of us.

Women and Stepfamilies reflects the diversity of women's experiences in stepfamilies. Not only does it represent the different positions or roles women hold in stepfamilies and the multiple variations that make up stepfamilies (number and ages of children, distances between parts of the families, and custody arrangements, to name a few), it also includes voices of women from many class, race, ethnic, regional, religious, and educational backgrounds and from different sexual orientations. Of course, we would like even more perspectives.[5] Many women are reluctant to write about their stepfamily situations, even when they are positive. Many of those who did write changed the names of the people involved, and some changed their own name or used only their first name. To write about the so-called private world of the family takes a kind of courage; writing about one's stepfamily, since it involves so many people, means risking a delicate network of relations.

We write to share our stories. We write, as Elizabeth Minnich says, "in this weave of common and different experiences" to uncover "some of the mysteries that still enshroud the real experience of motherhood as personal experience and as institution." We write to deconstruct the dominant myths about families and stepfamilies, to bear witness to our complicated family structures, and, as Catharine Stimpson suggests, to "seek to imagine new communities of intimacy."

Women and Stepfamilies is divided into three major sections: "Perspectives," "Stepping Out," and "Transforming—Both Within and Without." Part I, "Perspectives," consists of first-person narratives, interviews, stories, and poems about being in or being related to stepfamilies. The pieces in Part II are written by women who have chosen to *step out* of the intensity of their emotional lives and the subjective limits of being *in* families in order to reflect on stepfamily life. In Part III, "Transforming," many of the problems described and the questions raised in the first two sections are recast. These accounts describe stepfamilies that have used some of their feminist understandings to transform themselves, or at least work toward that transformation; some of these accounts offer a communal and social perspective on the functioning of families. Many of the pieces provide a liberating vision and grounds for hope for all women in stepfamilies.

Voices

Before the second wave of feminism in the 1960s and 1970s, families were assumed to have one perspective: that of the man, the so-called head of the household. Now we understand there are many perspectives in one family.[6] To those newly rediscovered voices of the "nuclear" family, *Women and Stepfamilies* adds those of the stepmother, the biological mother, the stepdaughter, the stepsister, and the stepgrandmother in a newer text of the family. All the articles in *Women and Stepfamilies* are from one or more of these perspectives; in fact the writer is often both a mother *and* a stepmother, or a daughter, a stepdaughter, *and* a stepsister. In lesbian stepfamilies the biological mother and the stepmother live together, not in separate families, offering a different perspective than when the biological mother and the stepmother are in two different but overlapping families. All these pieces deal with issues in the common dramas of daily life, most notably issues of love, identity, and power which often manifest themselves in struggles over space, time, and money. These issues are more complicated for the stepfamily because they are seldom acted out in one place and the players are seldom limited to just one immediate family.

A stepmother appears to be in an almost impossible position—at least until the process of interaction works itself out over years *and* until the stepmother unravels and resists the compulsory nature of the institution. For some, like Christine Bryson and Suzanne Bunkers, the concern is how to enter the step-relationship in the first place. Bryson's letters communicate a sense of being overwhelmed; she is transformed overnight from a part-time into a full-time stepmother.

What to call the stepmother is a repeated issue. Is she co-parent, the other mother, the "flommy" (in Clausen's novel *Sinking, Stealing*), the maid, a friend, a pal, or "slave cousin," as one woman (Wendy) ironically calls herself? Andrea Starr Alonzo does not use her step-title. This, she speculated, is related to her Afro-American heritage where children are valued as wealth, not solely in terms of biological relationships.

The stepmother's relation to her stepchildren is another puzzle. Kathleen Dunn, who has a son and a stepson, worries about favoritism. The writings of Carol Ascher, Deborah Rosenfelt, and Kathy Chamberlain ask how the stepmother maintains a relationship with the stepchild without the presence of her partner, the biological parent. Often the father is absent because of divorce, death, or separation. It is a more vexed question for the lesbian stepmother or the nonmarried stepmother. Sophia Carestia describes a stepmother who has infrequent contact with her stepdaughter and finds that contact always mediated first through the biological mother and then the biological father, with whom she lives. "The Barbie Doll Fight" describes the differences stepmothers and mothers have (even when they live together) over the bringing up of the child. Suzanne Bunkers, who was first a stepmother and then a mother, finds being a stepmother "ten times harder."

Many of the stepmothers are haunted simultaneously by the images of the wicked stepmother and the perfect (biological) mother. Helane Levine-Keating sees the biological mother in the children, in the husband, and in their shared history; Alice Neufeld tries to support her stepdaughter in her hungry desire to make contact with her biological mother.

In many ways mothers are the mirror (inverse) images of stepmothers, although stepmothers don't feel that to be true. Mothers worry about who the real mommy is if there is a stepmother and how to relate to this other woman. Sheila Alson records the first weeks of "one particular mother's experience with her children's acquisition of a stepparent." She wants to make contact with the stepmother but finds it hard: "I know none of her reactions. I know only my own and the reactions of my children, at least those they share with me." "Daisy Chain" underscores further the gulf between mother and stepmother and reaches for that which they have in common: "are we soul sisters or mortal enemies? " In "Step-by-Step Parenting," Dee, the mother, who lives with Wendy, the stepmother, describes how over a period of years, the mother can give up "ownership" of the child and share it with the stepmother, for the benefit of all. In "The Step-Wedding" the mother and the stepmother act out their familiar roles in old scripts, even though the families have been without contact for years. For children who live with their mother for some time, the arrival of a stepparent (and children) is seen as an intrusion; the mother must mediate between child and new lover (and the lover's family as well). Yandra Soliz says her daughter is angry, not only for being placed in a racially mixed family, but for having other people introduced into the solitary and intimate mother-daughter relationship.

Stepdaughters writing here certainly are angry. Lizzie Borden ("Lizzie's Axe") is the archetypal stepdaughter who kills her stepmother and her father. Samantha in the story "Mementos" is angry that her stepmother Lois has, upon her father's death, sold the family home in South Dakota and all their mementos. The story presents voices of both stepmother and stepdaughter. Their differences are most sharply felt around politics and lifestyle. But stepdaughters often want ways to make contact with their stepmothers; the act of going shopping or sharing clothes is charged for these women: "It was to be like you / that I tried all your clothes on." (Alison Townsend). Berenice Lopez and O. C. had differences with their stepfathers. Lopez admits long-pent-up anger toward both her stepfather and father for their indifference and their preference for other children. She had an extended family to comfort her, but it also provided the context of her abuse. O. C. came in conflict with her stepfather's discipline, yet also appreciated the different culture he brought to her mother and her.

Stepdaughters express much ambivalence toward the fact of having two "mothers." The title from Alison Townsend's diary entries captures that tension: "The Mother Who Isn't the Mother But Is." The stepdaughter interviewed by Elisa Davila felt herself the cause of internal tensions within two households and between two households. She was an intruder and obstacle both to her stepfather and her stepmother. Shirley Geok-Lin Lim's tension is not only familial but cultural in that expectations of stepmothers are different for Chinese and English culture. In these accounts, stepmothers and stepdaughters live uneasily with each other, although Hedva Lewittes describes three generations of stepwomen who struggle with that relationship through dialogue.

For stepsisters, having stepsiblings is often positive, although not without complications. Many of the complications come from outside the family. Erin Marie Hettinga says many white people believe her family to be abnormal. She lived with her white mother and black stepfather and his granddaughter, whom she considers her sister. For Hettinga, this complicated and variegated family enriches her life. While stepdaughters and stepsisters frequently express pain, anger, and jealousy in the early years of a stepfamily, in the later years they often come to voice a kind of appreciation for the members of their stepfamilies. One woman who corresponded with us, writes that she learned much as a stepsister from her family "tribe," as she calls it:

> If both these lessons—learning to relate to those not of my own kind, and learning to accept the human finitude of my parents—are essential lessons of growing up, then having a stepfamily helped me to learn them in a context that was loving, supportive, and never dull. As an adult, I am convinced that my relationship with my own mother has developed and grown as a result of our enlarged family. My mother and I have become friends, in part because the presence of the other family members has mediated our relationship in positive ways.

Perhaps one of the most overlooked aspects involves grandparents. Both the stepgrandmothers writing here receive much satisfaction from their interactions with their stepgrandchildren. Juanita Howard had little opportunity to be a stepmother to her husband's daughter; however, she was able to participate as a "stepgrandma" on a regular basis. Her conflicts were whether she would be a good enough stepgrandmother and how to balance her own professional schedule with the erratic scheduling of a stepfamily. Judith Higgs had opportunities to be a stepmother to her husband's fourteen children since their first mother had died; for her, instant motherhood and adoption of two of the children turned out to be nothing like television's Brady Bunch. Her positive story began when she became a stepgrandmother.

Howard and Higgs learned how to be a stepgrandmother in steps; both were first stepmothers. Many stepgrandparents, with no previous experience in stepfamilies, are at best awkward in their roles, at worst hostile to their nonbiological grandchildren. Wendy's stepdaughter (Dee's daughter) does not exist for Wendy's parents. While this might be explained as homophobia, stepchildren in heterosexual families also often go unacknowledged by grandparents. For stepmothers neither death nor divorce makes their entry into the family any easier. However, these accounts suggest that because stepgrandchildren do not have those divided loyalties that stepchildren usually feel, stepgrandmothers can be their friends rather than be trapped into trying to be a perfect mother-substitute.

Feminist Lens

When we read these accounts of women's stepfamily experiences through a feminist lens, themes emerge that raise questions about prevailing notions of motherhood and the family. In addition, what we learn about stepfamilies helps us rethink our feminism: we ask who and what is "mother"; what constitutes "family"; what rights and responsibilities do people have in families based on blood, caring, and economic contributions? These accounts challenge us to consider what is needed for women in stepfamilies to thrive and, at the same time, be connected to others in responsible and loving relationships.

Survival

For many women in stepfamilies, merely surviving the physical, economic, and emotional challenges of daily life is all-consuming. Berenice Lopez's account reflects the harshness of stepfamily life for women, and points to the lack of choices many women have. Similarly, Andrea Starr Alonzo's piece highlights how the struggle for economic survival shapes consciousness and behavior. These two selections underscore the privilege of women who have options to change their material situations, let alone step back, write about their experiences, and begin to work them through.

Even for women with desire, opportunity, and skills to step out of their situation to reflect on it, the emotional urgency of negotiating the complexities of lives in stepfamilies can supersede intellectual understanding and feminist consciousness. This emerges in several pieces, among them Sheila Alson's. Intellectually she is able to step out of her situation during a difficult transition period and gain perspective on it. Yet what she knows and what she feels are at odds. For example, she sees the value of developing a relationship with her ex-husband's new partner, but her overwhelming sense of sadness and loss prevents that. Thus, feminist insight— or any kind of reflective stance—while meaningful and clarifying, still may not match the power of the emotional experience.

Introduction

Much of the struggle of women in stepfamilies is to enable significant relationships to survive or to emerge in changing family structures. This can take many forms. Yandra Soliz, a mother, is torn by her child's pain at having to share her mother with a new stepfamily. The myriad losses to stepmother and stepdaughter in an aborted relationship are poignantly rendered in Kathy Chamberlain's piece. Sheila Alson articulates the generic fear of mother and children as they enter new stepfamily relationships: "Will I still be loved?"

Fitting into "The Family"

Prevailing ideas about the family have profoundly affected women. We have learned that in a family a woman is nurturer, the emotional linchpin for family members, and has primary responsibility for meeting others' needs. Many women try to succeed in stepfamilies by attempting to live up to these norms. While some women have found this workable, others have found it painful or self-defeating.

For some women the trauma of fitting into a newly formed family is minimized by cultural acceptance of this family form. As Andrea Starr Alonzo and Margaret Wade-Lewis point out, stepfamilies have always existed in black women's histories even though they were not necessarily named as such or talked about as unusual.

However, for many women, especially feminists, the expectation of fitting into traditional family forms is a source of profound conflict. Some women suddenly find themselves in stepfamilies where they are expected to experience this new reality as their "real family." Alison Townsend poignantly describes this from her point of view as a stepdaughter who, as a child, gained a stepmother soon after her own mother's death. Her initial resistance, refusing to call her stepmother "Mom," went unsupported. This sudden imposition of "The Family" laid the basis for years of pain in her simultaneous resistance and desire to bond with "the mother who is not the mother, but is."

Many of the women writing in this volume describe the trauma caused by trying to make the stepfamily an instant, traditional family. The implications for the stepmother are particularly overwhelming. When a stepmother attempts to fill the role of the "good mother," her efforts, destined by the structure of stepfamilies to be imperfect, merely confirm her wickedness. In most families the "good" biological mother cannot be replaced in children's hearts and minds and a stepmother's efforts at fulfilling this role breed resentment. Furthermore, when stepmothers do not meet

8

their internalized expectations of the unconditionally loving mother, they often blame and dislike themselves. Stepmothers find themselves afraid to discipline stepchildren or to engage in any meaningful interactions that might provoke conflict for fear of confirming their wickedness. Kathleen Dunn notes that similar comparisons between the "good father" and "wicked stepfather" are rare.

Elizabeth Kamarck Minnich suggests that the stepmother symbolizes for all of us the loss of the good mother, a loss beyond our control. It evokes our vulnerability and surfaces what we would like to forget: the contingency of human life. Ultimately, however, feminism suggests it will be women in stepfamilies who, in creating alternatives to the ideal of the good biological mother and the rightness of the traditional family, can challenge the power of those myths. It is in varied and diverse family forms that all members, especially women, can breathe, grow, and create relationships not limited by gender stereotypes.

Making Stepfamilies Work for Women

From these accounts we can learn what structural barriers stand in the way of women's thriving in stepfamilies and what can be done about them. The first step is to recognize the barriers.

Male power in families and patriarchal family forms keep women from raising issues about their roles as women in stepfamilies, from asking questions about why women's experiences in stepfamilies are comparatively more difficult and complex than men's, and from creating more diverse, equitable family arrangements. Christine Bryson won't talk openly about her concerns as a woman in a stepfamily because her husband believes these issues to be private; she appears here under a pseudonym. Under patriarchy, family issues are private, "under control" (male control) and not questioned.

For lesbians in stepfamilies, the power of the patriarchy is even more overwhelming. Despite years of loving parenting by lesbians co-parenting one partner's children, parental rights are defined by the male legal system using traditional family forms as the norm. Women describe the tension in their relationships generated by fear that their lesbianism will be discovered and custody of their children lost. This fear is often accompanied by the subtext of familial disapproval expressed through the judgment and distancing of grandparents, which increases the feelings of isolation for lesbians in stepfamilies.

Women's writing here also reveals the effects of racism and the boundaries of culture on their fulfillment in stepfamilies. The racism experienced by Soliz, for example, from both unknown others and extended family members weighed heavily upon her interracial stepfamily. In response to the racism in society and white attitudes about childrearing, the six step-mothers Wade-Lewis interviewed drew upon African American family traditions to strengthen their stepfamilies. For Shirley Geok-Lin Lim, Eastern and Western culture clashed, making painful her quest for identity and love in her stepfamily.

Constraints of class, as well, limit women in stepfamilies. In many areas of their lives, working class women have fewer options. Women enter, or stay in, stepfamilies for economic reasons, as Berenice Lopez and Elisa Davila point out. Because men, Judith Grant suggests, often keep women one foot out of poverty, they take on patriarchal authority in other family areas. So too, changes in family forms are far from the experience of many working-class people, for whom very little ever changes, Dympna Callaghan reminds us. Then again, some working-class families may historically have more experience with extended-family forms, so that stepfamilies are not felt to be problematic in the same way they are for some middle-class families.

Identifying such structural and cultural barriers to making stepfamilies work can help women stop blaming themselves for stepfamily problems and direct their emotions and actions toward creating change in the society that imposes these barriers. Meanwhile, living these lives, women can name these constraints on their family, attempt to challenge their limits, and where possible risk living in stepfamilies in self-defined ways. This book suggests those possibilities. Connie Miller speaks not only for herself but for many courageous women when she defines such a process of risk taking as "an act of resistance to external imperatives" that is necessary to the liberated, self-determined life and the hope for broader social and cultural transformation.

As we listen to the voices here, we can discern factors that have helped women live in stepfamilies with integrity. We come to see that family forming is a process that happens over time. Women with consciousness of the importance of this process, as compared to any received structure of The Family, express insight about their family's development. Dee and Wendy, for example, look back and identify important changes in the process of family forming; starting family rituals like the celebration of Chanukah; building on commonalities between stepmother and stepdaughter not shared by the mother; drawing boundaries around the adult relationship; and joining a lesbian parent support group.

Feminism provides critique, vision, and support for many of these writers. Catharine Stimpson finds feminist discourse to be "the most searching, steadfast, and sustaining" as she lives daily life with her stepchildren. Feminist values motivate Sarah Turner to be very intentional in creating cooperative, reciprocal, and equal relationships in her extended stepfamilies, especially between mother and stepfamily. Feminism offers women the consciousness and practical skills to join together, share with each other, and struggle creatively to transform their lives. One example is the stepmothers' support group that Nancy Schniedewind describes.

Nancy Schniedewind, Suzanne Bunkers, Sheila Alson, and Dee and Wendy have joined women's groups, not only because it is a place to discuss the problems of one's family, but because it is a place to create connections to other women so that sisterhood becomes a form of "familiness." While encouraging these personal and collective solutions, feminism also recognizes that broad-based societal change is ultimately necessary for the liberation of women in stepfamilies.

Transforming "The Family"

Rather than being limited by The Family, feminism has offered a vision of a broadened definition of family. Families can be living arrangements in which people share time and space, contribute equally to the physical and psychological tasks of making the household function, share common history and ritual, and make a commitment to staying together over time. Members are not necessarily tied by biology or by the sanction of state or church or by living in the same house all the time. All members seek both to give and receive support and love; all have space to grow as autonomous individuals. Stepfamilies, then, could be one of the many accepted family forms—no better or worse, no more normal or atypical than any other. In stepfamilies, we can learn to see families as changeable and affirm that fact. We can learn to expect the formation of a stepfamily as a normal life transition, just as now we expect a child will ultimately leave home. As we learn to expect a combination of sadness and renewal in the child's leaving, we can expect the same for changes in family forms.

Prevailing ideologies, based on myths of scarcity, have taught women that love is the special province of The Family, or stepfamily-become-Family. From these pages some women in stepfamilies attest to the strength of affiliation itself, rather than formal family ties, as the bond that sustains relationships. Stepmothers' fears of the loss of relationship with a stepchild after the end of the adult relationship exude from the pieces by Carol Ashner and Deborah Rosenfelt. Yet their desire and commitment to maintain that bond outside formal family structures confront these fears.

Stepfamilies can push women to value and act on their own needs as much as those of other family members. For example, stepmothers who have experienced the trap of attempting to be the "good" mother learn that they can separate from the family to develop themselves and, at the same time, be consciously connected to the family by sharing responsibility for its health. With one foot in and the other foot out, a stepmother can be both woman and parent. This position is often appreciated by other family members, as when Lewittes's stepdaughter characterizes their relationship as "happy detachment." This stance, which Elizabeth Minnich calls being a "conscious outsider," doesn't free women from pain, but does provide hope for wholeness of both women and families. Similarly, such families can help break down gender roles by compelling men to take on more of the parenting.

Because this volume presents women writing about their experiences in stepfamilies, men's voices are absent. Some women describe very positive, warm relationships with men, be they stepfathers, stepbrothers, or husbands. Yet other women here do not portray men as understanding or helping to resolve women's tensions in stepfamilies. Many of the women speak in voices edged with anger, bitterness, and unacknowledged hurt. A few women depict men as explicitly rejecting involvement because of notions of masculinity that encourage authoritarian roles or distancing behaviors. In other accounts, men are noticeably absent from women's descriptions of their struggles to negotiate the emotional turmoil of their lives. Once again, as in the traditional nuclear family, women seem to be the emotional linchpin of the family system.

As noted before, for men in stepfamilies, there is nothing comparable to the power of the socially imposed ideology of the "good mother" that drives women to taking this responsibility. Yet, because of the contradictions between lived experience and the ideology, women here articulate a feminist critique of the stepfamily, just as it was women who first articulated a critique of the nuclear family. Some men, from their own circumstances of having to take on sudden, new family roles and responsibilities, often first from divorce and then single active parenting, have developed a similar analysis. For men in stepfamilies, whose new roles have often created all-consuming practical and emotional tensions for them with family members, thus lessening the support they give to women, it is important that they take a first step and speak out from their various perspectives, so that they too can name their pain and claim their responsibilities.

Relationships among women pose both hard challenges and possibilities to women in stepfamilies. Linkages among women in the same stepfamily, especially between stepmother and mother, are often the most difficult. Our well-learned lessons of competing for a man and distrusting other women emerge. In her review of recent stepfamily fiction, Nan Bauer Maglin discovers that stepfamily stories exonerate men. Women in these works do not see each other as allies and sisters; rather the "other" is another woman—the other mother. Yet here in *Women and Stepfamilies* women's voices resonate with hopes for female bonding, even in awkward situations such as Morgan David's. Barbara Drucker and Sarah Turner document working relationships between stepmother and mother, founded on feminist consciousness. It is the political and social power society gives to *the mother* and denies to women in other spheres of their lives, Elizabeth Minnich reminds us, that works to separate woman from woman by relegating other women to second-class status.

Women in stepfamilies, therefore, have the potential for transforming both women's role as mother and the family itself. By relinquishing some of the power of motherhood (which we have only one step removed, if at all), we can relate more fully as women. By challenging the myth of biological motherhood we can help create diverse forms of family in which parenting is shared. By replacing the "good mother" with mature adult women, we can create the space for women concurrently to be autonomous and connected in loving relationships with others. By sharing our stories we can see our connectedness and catalyze change in the broader social fabric shaping our lives. With such revisioning and concomitant social action, families can then have the hope of becoming collectives of individuals, living democratically and cooperatively together, sharing responsibility, power, and love.

Notes

1. There are 35 million stepparents in America and 1,300 stepfamilies are formed every day. One out of every five children has a stepparent. By 1990 more people will be part of a second marriage than a first. These statistics, referred to in much of the stepfamily literature, probably do not include unmarried couples and surely do not include same-sex couples.

2. One recent book, *Stepmotherhood: How to Survive Without Feeling Frustrated, Left Out or Wicked* by Cherie Burns (New York: Times Book, 1985), clearly focuses on women but does not bring a feminist perspective to the subject. Burns includes quotes from women but only in excerpted form. While this is a very useful book, it assumes a fairly consistent white, middle-class heterosexual perspective on the whole. Many of the other books in the field (and there are now more coming out each year)—except for some few autobiographical ones like Patricia Tracy Lowe's *The Cruel Stepmother* (Englewood Cliffs, N.J.: Prentice-Hall, 1970), Mary Zenorini Silverweig's *The Other Mother* (New York: Harper and Row, 1982), and

Introduction

Delia Ephron's *Funny Sauce: Us, the Ex, the Ex's New Mate, the New Mate's Ex, and the Kids* (New York: Viking, 1986)—do not give full voice to the dense and variegated experiences of women in very different kinds of stepfamilies. For a fairly comprehensive bibliography of books and articles about stepfamilies, see Ellen J. Gruber, *Stepfamilies: A Guide to the Sources and Resources* (New York: Garland Publishing, 1986). *The Good Stepmother: A Practical Guide,* by Karen Savage and Patricia Adams (New York: Crown Publishers, 1988), has come out just as this book has gone to press.

3. See, for example, Joyce Trebilcot, ed., *Mothering: Essays in Feminist Theory* (Totowa, N.J.: Rowman & Allanheld, 1983); Barrie Thorne and Marilyn Yalom, eds., *Rethinking the Family: Some Feminist Questions* (New York: Longmans, 1982); and Irene Diamond, ed., *Families, Politics and Public Policy: A Feminist Dialogue on Women and the State* (New York: Longmans, 1983).

4. Dr. Elizabeth Stern is the wife of Dr. William Stern, the biological father of "Baby M." He fought for custody of Baby M from Mary Beth Whitehead, who is the biological mother of the baby, although she is termed the "surrogate mother."

5. *Women and Stepfamilies* begins to point to what must be a much more extensive exploration of commonalities and differences based on race, ethnicity, sexual preference, and class. Writers representative of "dominant" groups, whether white, heterosexual, or middle class, unfortunately focus less on the effects of these factors on their lives than do women of color, lesbians, or working-class women, whose survival necessitates such consciousness. Johnetta B. Cole, addressing the question of what U.S. women have in common and what their differences are, points out that, especially in terms of the family, that question is both complex and controversial. She advises that "we need . . . to listen to what women say about experiences in families as they vary by race, ethnicity, and by all other characteristics of family members. If we listen to what different women say about their experiences in their diverse family arrangements, we will acknowledge and come to understand that for women as a group, as well as for individual women, life in families is contradictory—involving restrictions, constraints, and oppressive acts on the one hand and support, protection, comfort, and indeed joy on the other" (*All American Women: Lines That Divide, Ties that Bind* [New York: The Free Press, 1986], p. 15).

6. Rayna Rapp, Ellen Ross, and Renate Bridenthal, "Examining Family History," *Feminist Studies* 5, (Spring 1979): 174–200.

References

Clausen, Jan. *Sinking, Stealing.* Trumansburg, N.Y.: Crossing Press, 1985.
Zipes, Jack. *Don't Bet on the Prince: Contemporary Feminist Fairy Tales in North America and England.* New York: Metheun, 1986.
Zipes, Jack. "Kissing Off Snow White," *New York Times Book Review,* March 22, 1987.

Part I

Perspectives

Stepmothers

I

Letters from a Custodial Stepmother

Christine Bryson

January 29, 1985

Dear Ms. Maglin:

On Saturday, January 26, I completely lost emotional control for the first time in my life and terrified my stepson, age twelve, and shocked my husband of five years. All I did was scream, but I was as shocked as everyone else was. My stepdaughter, age seventeen, is away at college. My husband's two children moved in with us two years ago because their mother was letting their stepfather abuse them and, after five sessions in court, my husband obtained their custody.

Last night, "stepfamily" problems almost got the best of me again. After my husband and I went to bed, he fell asleep and I was still fuming, so I got out of bed, padded quietly into our living room and very intently read the articles in my newest *MS.* magazine (February 1985) about the "blended family" (a term which is *too* polite, according to my way of thinking), hoping to find some help, reassurance, information, anything.

Unfortunately, the world is mostly dealing with custodial stepfathers and visitation stepmothers, and very few people even realize that there are those of us who are custodial stepmothers. I am writing today also to the Stepfamily Association for information and, hopefully, a support network for women in my unusual, but not unique, circumstance.

I found your request to hear from other stepparents about our experiences. Well, mine have been unusual and not all happy ones, although, in fairness, not all unhappy either. What do you want to know? Maybe if I tell someone, it will help.

Very truly yours,
Christine Bryson

February 12, 1985

Dear Nan,

I was so pleased to receive your response to my letter. I thought I'd take the opportunity to confirm my interest in working "with" you to help others in our situation if, in any way, I can.

As you may recall, I mentioned that I am a custodial stepmother, which is a somewhat unusual circumstance. Imagine my surprise when my office recently hired a woman who is also a custodial stepmother. She is only in her mid-twenties and has a fifteen-year-old stepdaughter, as well as a husband of almost five years and a two-year-old child of her current marriage. She and I have spent many moments together laughing and commiserating about those things in our "steplives" which are similar as well as those which are different. She, also, is looking for support. I gave her your letter to read this morning. Although her response was one of strong interest, she did not want to become involved.

To answer your letter: yes, I am interested in becoming involved. I, too, would like to know how much of this other people have been through and how much is uniquely mine to deal with. I suppose it would do my outlook some good to reflect on the good that "stepfamilying" has brought me. It is easy to dwell on the bad and get a sour attitude. You know, like when divorcees begin to think that all men are rotten. It is easy for me to think that all children are rotten and all fathers are rotten.

I think the book idea is wonderful. I can see how developing a network among those of us in this "situation" could be helpful in developing an understanding and disseminating information. I would be both frightened and excited to feel I might be a part of something that will affect other's lives. However, I will echo your thought that perhaps I should begin all this just by writing you letters. I need to think it all out. Right now I'm too angry to have much to say that is constructive.

You mentioned the fact that your daughter and others around you have been affected already by your writing. I hope that you will not feel so panicked and guilty that you end your efforts on our behalf. Perhaps if we were all required to be so honest with those around us, they would understand better and deal with the inevitable hurt more quickly. As you may have realized by now, I do not have the "guts" (interpret "honesty"?) to even let my own family know that this issue bothers me so much that I have to look for support. That is the reason why our dealings, for now at least, have to be through my office address. My husband does not like people to talk about personal issues to "outsiders." Neither to him nor about him.

I remember vividly the day that I had "had it up to here" (see my hand at my forehead) and ran to the local library for answers. I brought home a stack of books and before I could open one, my stepdaughter was all over them jokingly accusing me (and there is much truth in jest, is there not?) of having problems with being a stepmother.

I will take some time and gather my thoughts as to the things that I really want to speak out about. Then, perhaps I can write to you little by little and deal with each subject.

It's good knowing someone is trying to do something about all of this mess which our contemporary lifestyles have brought us. If I can be of help, let me. If I hinder the process, be honest enough to tell me. Thank you for your support. I hope your daughter is, by now, beginning to understand.

Very truly yours,
Christine

April 10, 1985

Dear Nan,

I think of your research often, particularly when talking with other "blended-family" members. I wonder how you are doing and what you are hearing from all the other people in the world. Lots of ideas have gone through my mind since we last "talked." There are so many things I want to say. Of course, in the heat of passion, one tends to act and react more quickly. When I first wrote to you in reaction to the articles in *MS.* magazine, I was reacting to a very bad event at home with my "blended family." As time has passed, things have once again become more quiet. However, the issues are still there. They have not changed and they have not disappeared.

I think it's about time I start to put some of my ideas into words. If not to aid in your research, then just to help myself sort them out by forcing them into black and white.

One of my biggest gripes, although I have so many, is the fact that I had no choice in becoming a custodial stepmother (for sake of ease in typing, can we call her a CSM?). That is a major difference between most CSMs and most custodial stepfathers (CSF). I believe, though I have no numbers to support my belief, that most men become CSFs by marrying women who already have custody of their own children. I doubt that many men become CSFs some time *after* they marry. Most women get custody and retain custody of their children during divorces. They don't begin *without* custody and gain custody after a subsequent marriage. So the man that marries her knows up front that he will become a CSF on saying "I do."

Women who become CSMs—more often than men, I think—do so some time *after* they say "I do," as the "real" mother has custody from the divorce but for some reason voluntarily or involuntarily loses it. How many men get custody of their children when they are single? So a woman marries a man expecting the typical every-other-weekend-visitation life, but, for whatever reason, the father gets custody and the "new" wife becomes a CSM.

Take my situation, for example. Gary (my husband) and Susan (his first wife and the mother of his children) had two children together. They had an amicable divorce. Of course she got the children. He didn't even try. She remarried. The new husband (David) knew he was going to become a CSF before he married her. He knew what was in store for him and he had an opportunity to make a choice. Gary and I married at about the same time. During Susan and David's marriage, Gary found out that David was very badly abusing the children and Susan was letting him. Gary's visitation was affected as well. So Gary took it to court to have the visitation problem fixed. As time went on, Gary learned more and more about the abuse and he finally asked the court for custody, not just visitation.

At that point, we had been married about two years. We had determined before we were married that we would not have children. Neither one of us wanted them. I've never wanted children. I'm not the nurturing type. He'd already been through it.

When we started talking about getting custody of his kids, I couldn't very well say "no" could I? I could not leave them in that terrible situation. I may not be the nurturing type, but I am compassionate. The choice was to leave the two kids where they were being beaten, malnourished, and psychologically abused, or for me to become a CSM. Sure, at one point Gary asked me if I was willing and I had the opportunity to say "no." Fat chance. That would essentially give the man a position of having to choose between his wife of a few years and his blood children. He would have to have chosen between being married to me and knowing he left his children in a terrible situation, or being a single father. As Joan Rivers says, "Oh, grow up!" You know the choice I had was no choice and the choice he would have had would have been no choice.

I've mentioned in my earlier letters that one of my co-workers is a CSM. She married her husband knowing he had one child from his first marriage, but the child was in the mother's custody. They did not expect to ever gain custody. They married with the intent to have "their own" family (she is now in her mid to late twenties, he is in his mid-thirties). She gave birth two years ago to a little boy. Shortly after that, her husband felt compelled to gain custody of his daughter from his first marriage as her home situation had become very bad. My friend and her husband have had custody now of his daughter for two years. The daughter is now sixteen years old. What choice did my friend have?

I liken it in my own mind to changing the rules in the middle of a very important game. It makes me angry. But my hands are tied, as are the hands of probably most of the other custodial stepmothers in the world.

And to top it off, we CSMs are expected, just because we have female sex organs, to become the primary caretaker and nurturer of these step-children. A CSF, on the other hand, is not expected to be the primary caretaker or nurturer of his stepchildren, is he? Hell, no. But that's another subject. So I'll drop it here for now.

What do you think?

Very truly yours,
Christine

10-11-85

Dear Nan,

Just time for very quick note.

I too have had a tough summer. Back to court on the custody of Kurt, Gary's twelve-year-old (we kept him). Lynn, his seventeen-year-old and a sophomore in college, got pregnant so we dealt with the abortion issue firsthand. Gary was fired from his job. Life in the fast lane.

I now am the proud owner of a well-deserved new ulcer. Other than that, I've weathered it all well. I'm okay. I've been running. I've applied to work at a local college so I can take classes easier and get to work on my degree. For now though, I'm still at the firm. Gary does not know about this book, so the only chance I have to write is at work. That makes it tough.

But if you'll still listen, I'll still talk, 'cause I have a lot to say.

Must run—but know that I'm still out here stepmothering!

Until later,
Christine

January 30, 1986

Dear Nan,

It has been one year and one day since I first wrote to you. It has been over three months since I last wrote you and ten months since I last gave you anything of substance. And I am, honestly, feeling very guilty about the extreme passage of time.

Unfortunately, this letter has to be a mere contact, nothing much more because I have so little time. But I did want to let you know that I care very much about your project. I wonder how it is going for you.

I still have not told Gary about my contact with you. I wonder if I ever will. So that rules out doing anything out of the office as he is a very devoted husband and is with me or near me virtually all the time. He doesn't enjoy going out without me, so where I am, there he is also. It's flattering, but somewhat in the way at times. I have no opportunity to write during office hours. I rarely can get to the office early or stay late as Gary and I drive to and from work together. Tonight, however, due to "family responsibilities," we were forced to take separate cars, and I told him I had to stay and work overtime. Lunches I am usually busy running (literally) or running errands. It all sounds like excuses. I don't mean it to. Actually, they are merely reasons, although I feel guilty about it and wonder if perhaps I felt better about it all I would *find* time to write.

So, bottom line, I am still out here and still interested and wondering if you are still able to take contributions. Please forgive me for being so slow in writing.

Before I go, one story I have wanted to share with you for a long time.

A few years ago, before I was a custodial stepmother, I had the time to take an art class after work (I am slowly but surely getting my degree in art). During that semester, Gary and I were going through a very trying period with the kids. He had lost visitation rights and had absolutely no contact with either of his children for some time. Their mother refused his telephone calls and his letters were returned. The kids were about thirteen (Lynn) and eight (Kurt) years old.

One day, clear out of the blue, a counselor from Lynn's school called Gary at work and told him Lynn wanted to talk to him and would he be willing to talk to her. He was overjoyed, and, to make a long story short, within a few days, she was living with us. She had not told her brother what she was going to do as she did not want to burden him with the knowledge and the decisions that would accompany that knowledge. Her mother refused her any contact with her brother (with whom she had always been very close) after Lynn moved in with us.

It was a very awkward time for all three of us as we were happy that Lynn was with us, but so concerned about Kurt and his well-being. There seemed to be a very distinct gap or something missing—obviously it was Kurt.

Prior to all of this, back when things were going smoothly and the kids lived with their mother and we had regular visitation, Gary and I had set our camera up on a tripod, and had taken a photograph of the four of us on our front porch. It was a wonderful picture, full of wonderful feelings (if I can find a spare copy at home tonight, I'll send it to you).

Back to the story at hand. In my painting class, the teacher suggested we paint something that had a very strong, personal feeling for each of us. Right away I knew what I wanted to paint. That photograph, exactly as it was, with Kurt missing. Just a big white blank piece of canvas where his little body was in the photograph. I don't know why, but that was such a strong image. I had to paint it. I was really excited about it. It was just going to be such a strong statement that I felt many people would understand and relate to, whatever their personal perspective might be.

I came running home and excitedly told this idea to Gary. He was devastated! The image, the concept of the finished painting, was too much for him to bear. Although I certainly had the freedom to go ahead with my plan, I just could not do that to him. I didn't want to lie to him about what I was painting, and I didn't want to show him the painting when it was finished. But I would be too excited to not show it to him. So, out of deference to his strong, sad feelings, I never painted the picture. The image, however, still remains in my mind.

I wonder if there ever will be a day when he can step far enough away from all the horrible things that have happened to not be hurt by such a painting.

Well, time flies and it's about time I get out of the office. Let me know if you still want to hear from me.

Sincerely,
Christine

PS: Just a quick final note to let you know that the recent disasters in my life seem to be in check. Gary started working again in November and seems to be happy with this new position. Kurt's mother has moved out to Ohio and will have a much more difficult time pulling the little shitty things she used to try. Kurt is doing very well and appears to be much more stable now that the last court battle over his custody is finished. He was told by the judge that it would not be brought back into court unless Kurt asked for it (his mother nearly shit bricks!). Lynn pulled through the abortion like a trooper, as did Gary. I was very proud of his supportive attitude. We took her to a clinic together and sat in the waiting room together. My ulcer is now under control. I'm still running. Hoping next year to do my first marathon! I applied to work at a local college so I can take classes easier, but to date, they have not contacted me. I write them on a regular basis. Some day they'll give in just to get me off their backs. So I'm still at the firm. Happy enough. Not ecstatic with my life, but happy enough.

11/28/86

Dear Nan,

No time for details now. Wonder how the book is coming. I'm leaving my job at the firm. Going to work at the university—they'll let me take some day classes and pay my tuition! Some day I'll have a degree: masters in fine art.

Stepparenting still good/bad. As the years pass, we get more used to one another—thank God! Hope all is well with you.

Until later,
Christine

September 10, 1987

Dear Nan,

I'm "working late" tonight to take the time and review the letters you returned to me for my "editing." Please note the name changes. I obtained these names and places by literally opening a phone directory and putting my finger down on the pages! Anything "creative" I could think of, Gary could figure out. Even with all that, though, obviously if he ever read it all, he would know right away that was us. I'm just hoping that changing the names and places will keep anyone else around here from pointing it out to him.

I feel so odd about all of this. I'm sure that is part of the reason for my lack of letters to you. I feel I am betraying my best friend, and in a way I guess I am. Gary is my best friend and these are things I cannot be honest about with him. He also takes such great offense if anyone talks to anyone else about anything personal. I'm sorry for him that he doesn't develop a friendship so deep that he would talk about these kinds of feelings. But in the meantime, I simply don't let him know that there are a few special people I *do* talk to. You being one of them.

You know, in looking over the correspondence, I am surprised at how little there was from me. I must have thought so much more to say to you, or perhaps I started letters and never finished them. Anyway, I expected volumes of letters that I had written to you, though I am sure this is all there is. I find it all very hard to talk about. Also I find it very difficult to take time out of my life to do this. It's a circular or Catch 22 situation in so many ways.

I never told you about the chemistry or sexual rivalry (over Gary) between my stepdaughter and me when she first moved in. I never told you what life was so horribly like during the two years of going in and out of court and the way the kids treated their father and the way he continued to love them knowing it was their mother manipulating them and not their true feelings. I never told you about their relationship with their mother at this point in time.

I never told you that one thing that really gets under my skin is that when "grandparents" are talked about as far as sending school photos to them and the like, my parents are never even considered.

I never told you how angry/embarrassed I get when he jumps on the kids "on my behalf" when they are kidding me or something like that.

I never told you how hurt I've been by the thousands of little things over the years done to me or around me or because of me—the custodial stepmother. The wicked stepmother.

I never told you that I'm really a nice stepmother. I never told you that I love the kids and they love me and they've never once refused to do anything I've told them and they've never said to me, "You're not my mother!"

I've never told you that I count the years and days until we are once again the couple we were before we got custody of the kids.

I've never told you about what it feels like to be called to the hospital because one of the kids has been hurt and to have the hospital question my authority to sign for medical action "because you're not their mother, even if your husband has custody," and so now I go to the hospital and say I'm their mother and the kids look at me knowing I'm lying and wanting to say something but being in too much pain to raise hell.

I've never told you about the things the kids have confided in me or I've done with or known about the kids and don't tell their father because I don't think he'd be fair 'cause he can't be as objective as I am. I've never told you that I can see the kids objectively for what they are and where they are in life and their father sees them only as his little baby children, as his mother still sees him in spite of his forty years on this earth.

I've never told you how often I've thought of walking out on him 'cause I just can't take it any more, but afraid to walk out because of the damage it may do to the kids. Afraid to walk out because of the way his mother adores me after taking in the kids and treating them so well and loving them so much. Knowing I can't hurt all those "innocent bystanders" just because I "can't take it" for a few more years till the kids are grown and gone.

I've never told you that I had my tubes tied. And how I am sometimes worried that I will regret that decision when I am old and alone and have no family, but how my husband corrects me and reminds me that I *do* have children who will be there for me when I am old. And how I wonder if these two kids, who are not bone of my bone or flesh of my flesh, will really care anything about me when I am old and alone.

And how sometimes I wish nuclear families were still the rule and not the exception and life was like *Leave It to Beaver*. And how guilty I feel that I'm not home when Kurt comes home from school and that I don't fix him breakfast or lunch. And how guilty I feel when he comes home from school and wants to talk and I know it will bore me and I want to tell him, but I know how it would damage his tender emotional state and so I listen and resent it and resent him. And how guilty I feel that I don't spend time with Kurt. And how guilty I feel that I don't write letters to

Lynn and try to hide when she calls on the phone 'cause I don't really know what to talk about with her, even after all these years.

It's all so fucking depressing! I guess that's why I didn't write you tons of letters.

I've never told you how angry but powerless I feel when their father brings home white bread and Oreos and cola and gives it to them like a reward. And they gain weight. And they complain about the weight. But they like the food and Gary likes to see them enjoy life. But I'm a health food person who feels she has no power or authority, because, after all, they're not my kids. They're his kids to raise as he likes.

I've never told you that it makes me feel powerless that they are his kids to raise as he likes and that I really get no vote.

I've never told you that I am glad we did not have kids together because I so strongly disagree with the way he raises kids. Though he is, without a doubt, an excellent father, very loving and very kind. And I've never told you that he doesn't drink and I love him very much for that. My father was an alcoholic. My first husband was an alcoholic. And I refuse to ever live like that again.

I've never told you that my husband is my best friend, loving, kind, gentle, sexy, happy, warm. That my marriage is one of the best, most stable, I've ever seen.

I tend to go on and on with the negative making my life look awful. But I am really a very lucky woman, finding a wonderful man the second time around, falling into children and being lucky enough to get two that are honest, loving, kind, bright, trustworthy, fun, instead of the stereotypical stepchildren.

At least I know that by my not having children, I will never force another woman to become an unwitting custodial stepmother! (Of course, though, I sometimes dream of making a baby in my belly and going through delivery and raising it perfectly. Strictly an emotional, occasional, pull. Intellectually I know I am far too selfish and directed in my own life to really be a good mother or want to be a mother. But I digress . . .)

So my arms are around you and your co-workers and your brave "blended family" and all the other "steps" in the world, be they mothers, fathers, children, grandparents, cousins, anything. Maybe this book will be the line thrown to other drowning custodial stepmothers of this contemporary world.

With my deepest admiration,
Christine

2

Ten Times Harder: Becoming a Stepmother

Suzanne L. Bunkers

> Stepmothers-to-be usually have one of three popular precon-
> ceptions about stepmothering: (1) our stepchildren won't really
> be part of our marriage and lives; (2) our relationship with
> our stepchildren will be close and familial—like one big happy
> family; (3) we will love our stepchildren as though they were
> our own children. With a little experience we realize that all
> three beliefs are unrealistic.
>
> —Cherie Burns, *Stepmotherhood*

A few years ago, I had no idea that I would soon be facing the challenges
of stepmotherhood. In May 1984 I was living by myself in Mankato, Min-
nesota, where I had been teaching English and women's studies courses at
Mankato State University for the previous four years. I had been divorced
for over six years. I was feeling content to be on my own, with just my
cats, Vincent and Alice, as living companions.

From time to time I mused about what it might be like to be in another
relationship, particularly with someone who already had children, since,
at the age of thirty-four, I had none. Occasionally I felt an urge to do
some mothering. Stepmothering, I imagined, would be the easiest way to
fulfill this urge. I could spend some time around a child and not have to
be responsible for its daily needs, and I could get back in touch with that
childlike part of myself that had somehow gotten lost over the years as I
had focused my energies on my education and career.

My childhood in an alcoholic family and my own brief marriage at the
age of twenty-one had left me leery about any commitments to long-term
relationships or to the raising of children. My involvement in the feminist

movement had begun as a reaction to my realization that I had been overly responsible, both in my family of origin and in my marriage, for taking care of others. For several years I had been an active member of a women's support group, and I had recently completed codependency treatment. Both experiences had helped me to recognize that I needed to stop trying to "help" others by attempting to control their lives.

So, when I began a relationship with Randy that summer of 1984, I vowed to be careful to keep it light. Still, as the two of us grew closer, I felt more confident in my ability to make that relationship healthy. I felt both excited and apprehensive about the prospect of getting to know Randy's six-year-old son, Christopher. Randy and his former wife, Pat, shared custody of Christopher, who was with Randy during the school year and with Pat and her husband, Patrick, during the summer.

My first glimpse of Christopher was of a blond little boy in striped polo shirt and shorts, hiding behind Randy's legs as his father urged him to come out and meet me. The three of us went roller skating with friends that day, and I took a liking to Christopher when, at the skating rink, he confided in me that he really *was* scared of falling but was trying to make it look as if he wasn't. His words reminded me of what I had been like as a child—a scared little kid always trying to be brave. Later, when Randy told me about having gone through treatment for alcoholism two years prior to our meeting, I began to understand better that, as children of alcoholics, Christopher and I were bound to have feelings and behaviors in common.

I didn't see much of Christopher during the summer of 1984 because he spent most of it at his mother and stepfather's home in Iowa. In the fall, Randy, Christopher, and I had our first outing as a threesome. We went to the Twin Cities, where I cared for Christopher while Randy ran in a marathon. The whole day, Christopher kept his distance from me, pulling away when I tried to take his hand before crossing the street and running off at the finish line to fight his way through the crowds to Randy. Randy showed little affection toward me with Christopher present. I came away feeling hurt and disappointed. As the three of us drove back to Mankato that evening, I realized that I needed to think more seriously about what continuing my relationship with Randy would mean.

For one thing, it would mean that Christopher would be a central factor in how Randy and I interacted because Christopher would almost always be present. Randy and I would have very little time alone together, usually only late at night after Christopher would be asleep or on the two weekends a month he would visit his mother and stepfather. For another thing, it would mean that I would have to realize Randy's responsibilities as a single parent and that I would have to make some adjustments in my own expectations about relationships.

Before, I had always been in relationships with people who, like me, had no children and who could spend as much time with me as the two of us wished. I wasn't used to being around children. The last child I had cared for on a daily basis was my youngest brother, Dan, who had started kindergarten the year I left home for college. After about an hour of being with Christopher, I had had enough time together, yet I found I couldn't say, "Okay, go away now. I've had enough interaction for today." I had to recognize that I couldn't turn Christopher's presence on and off at will.

Randy didn't understand my discomfort and frustration when I explained my feelings to him. I found it difficult to be in the midst of a conversation with Randy, only to be interrupted as Christopher tried to get his father's attention. I found it disconcerting to be overheard by a six-year-old, but I felt guilty about complaining. What right did I have? Randy and Christopher, I told myself, had a preexisting relationship. When I entered the picture, it was up to me to fit in as best I could.

I knew that this was unhealthy, codependent thinking, yet I kept silent for several months. An unexpected turn of events brought my anger (and my underlying fears) to the surface: in March 1985 I found out that I was pregnant. An earlier tubal pregnancy and the diagnosis of severe endometriosis had led me to believe that I couldn't have a child, so this news was a shock—but not an entirely unwelcome one. I started to feel excited. I was going to have a child of my own! Randy seemed ambivalent about the prospect of becoming a father again, since he had expected that Christopher would be his only child. We would become a family, I told myself. It all sounded so easy and so right.

How would Christopher react to the news of my pregnancy? When Randy and I told him, Christopher seemed to like the idea. I felt relieved yet anxious when Christopher kept referring to the baby as his half-brother or sister. I wondered how he would adjust to no longer being the center of attention. I worried about how I would adjust to becoming a mother and a stepmother at virtually the same time. I agonized over what the coming changes would mean for my relationship with Randy. At the heart of my feelings was my fear that I was, and would remain, an outsider as far as Randy and Christopher's relationship was concerned. I decided to talk things over with Randy.

Our talk didn't go well. Randy was angry and defensive when I told him that I wanted his and my relationship to be the primary one, that I wasn't willing to put up with Christopher's demands for Randy's attention at my expense, that I wanted the dynamics of our relationship as a threesome to change before our baby was born. Like Randy, I felt defensive and angry. Would our baby and I have to take a back seat to the relationship between Randy and Christopher? I had gone from rarely seeing Christopher at the start of my relationship with Randy to being with him nearly all the time. I was scared. I knew that I didn't feel the unconditional love for Christopher that a "real" mother feels for her child. What could I do? How could I tell Randy that I didn't love his son? What would it be like when my own child was born? What if I couldn't even love my own baby?

In June 1985 Christopher left for two months at his mother and stepfather's. Shortly before, I had asked his stepfather, Patrick, if he ever felt invisible when he was with Christopher and his mother, Pat. Yes, Patrick had replied, early in his relationship with Christopher's mother, he had had to deal with exactly what I was experiencing—that feeling of being invisible, of being an outsider, not a part of the parent-child relationship. Patrick assured me, just as the women in my support group had, that things would get better as Christopher and I got to know each other better. But such reassurances were of little comfort. I didn't want to have to wait for months or even years. At the heart of my impatience, I later realized, was my fear that things might *never* change, that I might never feel anything for Christopher and that he might never feel anything for me.

That summer was one of the most painful I can remember. Randy and I tried to sort out what our relationship and living arrangements would be in the fall when Christopher returned and our baby was due. We made plans to move to the same town and share a house. Slowly we began to let go of some of the control that each of us had exercised over our own living situations up to that point. We had many intimate, angry, and poignant moments. In August we moved into one dwelling. Books, dishes, silverware, furniture spilled everywhere as we struggled to blend two households into one and create some semblance of a home.

Christopher, who had returned from his mother and stepfather's just days after Randy and I had unpacked our belongings, was shy and wary about being in a new town, making friends in a new neighborhood, and starting second grade at a new school. Those first weeks of September were miserable ones for me. Eight months pregnant, I couldn't sleep at night; I couldn't lift or carry things. I wondered about the approaching labor and delivery. Randy, who had been laid off from work, was anxious about the prospect of continued unemployment. Christopher stayed in the house, scared to go out and meet the neighborhood kids. When he tried to make friends with my cats, they hissed and ran away. It was an excruciating time for all of us. My way of dealing with the problems in our newly blended family was to reassure myself that as soon as the baby was born, everything would be all right.

Life with a seven-year-old unnerved me at times. I felt exasperated when Christopher left lights on, clothes and toys strewn about the room, a trail of Cheerios across the kitchen floor. By the final days of my pregnancy, I was wrung out. I fantasized about bringing the baby home to a house in which her father, she, and I could become a family. I wanted to savor the experience of having my first child. Christopher's presence was a constant reminder to me that this baby was not Randy's first child and that she would not be special in the same way to him as she would be to me.

On the other hand, I thought, perhaps having my own child would help me feel more loving toward Christopher. I hesitated to show affection for him because I feared that he could continue to pull away from me. I avoided disciplining him because I worried that, if I did, he would view me as a "wicked stepmother."

Randy's and my unmarried status also caused me some anxiety. To me, our status reinforced my fears that I could not become a stepmother to Christopher, that I was merely a "pretender" to the role.

One afternoon in mid-October my amniotic sac burst, and I told Randy that we'd need to go to the hospital that evening. At this news, Christopher burst into tears: "No! I don't want the baby to be born tomorrow!"

I turned to him: "I don't think *you're* going to decide when this baby will be born." Christopher cried even harder. Finally, I understood what was troubling him. His second-grade class was to go to the Minneapolis zoo the next day, and he was afraid that, if the baby were born, he wouldn't be able to go. Once reassured, he calmed down, and Randy and I left for the hospital after a good friend arrived to stay with Christopher.

Rachel Susanna was born the following day, October 17, 1985, after a difficult labor that culminated in a caesarean delivery. Despite my exhaustion, I was elated at having a daughter. I took great delight in responding to people's frequent question "Is this your first child?" with a cheerful nod and a recitation of Rachel's fine points. I was brought up short, however, the first time Randy was present when that question was asked. "No, I have a seven-year-old son," he replied. I felt silenced, diminished, and once again reminded that Randy and I were not sharing in the wonder of welcoming our first child into the world.

I wish I could say that the months following Rachel's birth were easy ones. I wish I could affirm that, as soon as the baby was born, everything *was* fine. But it wasn't. I recovered from the caesarean quickly, and Rachel was as good-natured an infant as I could have imagined. While my family and friends made much of Rachel's arrival, it seemed to me that Randy hung back, hovering over Christopher, trying to make sure that he didn't feel excluded. With every present Rachel received, it seemed that Christopher pointed out he hadn't gotten one. Whenever a visitor held Rachel and remarked on what a lovely baby she was, it seemed that Christopher diverted attention from his sister to himself. I wondered, would Rachel and I be shoved into the background?

I devoted even more attention to Rachel, with whom I felt the kind of mother-child bond that I didn't feel with Christopher. Would I have felt more love for him if he had been a girl, I asked myself? No, I didn't think so. My feelings for him had to do with the constant reminders that he had a mother elsewhere, a mother who was giving to him and getting from him the kind of love and attention that I wasn't.

During those first stressful months after Rachel's birth, when the four of us were starting to coalesce as a family despite Randy's unemployment, his mother's unexpected death, and my return to full-time teaching, Christopher had some very hard times. I am sorry to say that, in my attempts to create order out of what seemed like chaos, I gave him less attention than he deserved. It wasn't that I wanted to push him away, but he appeared to hold himself at a distance from me. Meanwhile, Randy devoted more attention to Christopher as I became more attached to Rachel. My relationship with Randy started to crack from the strain. We gave one another the silent treatment and accused one another of not caring about either our relationship or the family we had created.

Things continued like this until June 1986, when Christopher went to his mother and stepfather's for the summer, I began a year's sabbatical from teaching, Randy found work, and Rachel grew out of infancy. For the first time in many months, I could sit back, catch my breath, and reflect on things. Did I want the situation to continue as it had been? I knew that the answer was no. What, then, was I willing to do to change my own attitudes and behaviors? A good deal of hard and painful work with an excellent feminist therapist helped me to remember what I had learned in codependency treatment: as the oldest of five children in an alcoholic family, I had learned early how to take control of situations, care for the needs of others, and discount my own needs and desires. All these tendencies had come to dominate my daily interactions, particularly with Randy and Christopher. It was also painful to admit to myself that, while I had chosen to undertake responsibility for Rachel, I hadn't made so conscious or willing a choice about Christopher.

With the help of my therapist and women's support group, I made a key discovery: one reason why my relationship with Christopher was so problematic was that he reminded me of what I had been like as a child— sensitive, inquisitive, strong-willed, and so terrified of making mistakes and being criticized that I would withdraw in silence rather than risk possible rejection by any adult. It was time to face my feelings about my own past.

Now, two years later, I'm tempted to report that my relationship with Christopher has resolved itself into sweetness and light. Of course, that's not the way real life works. I still have times when I'm angry and resentful, times when I'm guilty and apologetic. I've learned to let myself experience my feelings—whatever they might be—and to name them, both to myself and to others.

For me, becoming a stepmother has been ten times harder than becoming a mother. Randy's and my attempts to create an "instant family" erupted into chaos immediately rather than slowly, forcing us to face issues that might otherwise have simmered for a long time before heating up to boiling. We continue to work on resolving these issues, with the recognition that the process is going to take a long time.

As for me, I can now see that there are rarely true villains or heroes in a stepfamily situation. I'm learning how to operate not out of anger, guilt, or shame but out of an honest acceptance of the ways in which my own fears of rejection underlie not only my conscious thoughts and actions but also those that are subconscious. As someone who has always prided myself on being "in control," I'm discovering that it's sometimes excruciatingly hard to drop that mask of control and let my real feelings surface, especially if they are feelings of sadness, anger, or fear. Yet that is exactly what I most need to do.

One day not long ago, when Christopher and I were home alone, he got out his album of baby pictures. We laughed as we looked at snapshots of him learning to sit up, crawl, walk, and play. We marveled at how much his little sister Rachel (whom he never calls his half-sister) looks like him. One photograph showed Christopher as a toddler, posing with his mother and his father. "You know, Suzanne," he said, "I don't remember anything about ever living with both my mom and my dad."

I wanted to cry. Suddenly Christopher looked very little and vulnerable. I put my arms around him, stroked his hair, and we sat there like that for quite a while. Finally I told him, "Your dad and I both love you. Your mom and Patrick do, too." Then he got up and put the photograph album away.

Little moments like that give me great hope for the future of my relationship as stepmother and stepson. I understand—and I accept—that I will never be Christopher's mother and that he will never be my son. I feel very sad and also tremendously relieved to have come to that realization, thanks, in good part, to my growing understanding of the ways in which my embracing of feminist parenting strategies, along with my movement away from codependent ones, is helping me establish a relationship with Christopher that is based not on control but on acceptance. It's important for me to know that the relationship we are establishing will benefit our family as a whole and each of us as an individual.

It has helped me, too, to read what Elizabeth Einstein (1985, p. 192) has noted about the realities of stepmothering:

> I was not a wicked stepmother offering my stepchildren poisoned fruit and dressing them in rags. Often I had to make decisions these youngsters disliked. All parents must; it is part of loving and responsibility. Loving my stepchildren differently from my own sons was not rooted in malice, but in the kind of human bonding that took place within the relationships.

For me, stepmothering involves much hard work. It involves a good deal of stumbling and hesitation. It involves some anger, fear, and guilt. And it involves equal portions of respect, hope, and love.

Epilogue

Spring 1988: Since I first wrote this essay, I've come to understand more about how alcoholism and other addictions have shaped the ways in which our stepfamily has functioned and have contributed to the problems discussed in this essay. The problems have proved to be too great. Randy and I are no longer together. Rachel and I have been living in Brussels, Belgium, while I am on a Fulbright grant. When we return to Mankato several months from now, I hope to continue my relationship with Christopher, though in a different kind of living situation.

References

Beattie, Melody. *Codependent No More.* Center City, Minn.: Hazelden Foundation, 1987.

Berman, Claire. *Making It as a Stepparent: New Roles, New Rules.* 2d ed. New York: Harper & Row, 1986.

Burns, Cherie. *Stepmotherhood: How to Survive Without Feeling Frustrated, Left Out, or Wicked.* New York: Harper & Row, 1985.

Clarke, Jean Illsley. *Self-Esteem: A Family Affair.* Minneapolis, Minn.: Winston Press, 1978.

Dreikurs, Rudolf, and Vicki Soltz. *Children: The Challenge.* New York: Hawthorn/Dutton, 1964.

Einstein, Elizabeth. *The Stepfamily: Living, Loving and Learning.* Boston: Shambhala Publications, 1985.

Jarmulowski, Vicki. "Blended Families: A Growing American Phenomenon . . . Who are They?" *Ms.* 13, no. 8 (February 1985): 33–34.

Maddox, Brenda. *Step-Parenting: How to Live With Other People's Children.* London: Unwin Paperbacks, 1980. (Originally published as *The Half Parent,* London: Andre Deutsch, 1975.)

Maglin, Nan Bauer. "It Could Not Be More Complicated." *Ms.* 13, no. 8 (February 1985): 40, 45.

Seixas, Judith S., and Geraldine Youcha. *Children of Alcoholism: A Survivor's Manual.* New York: Harper & Row, 1985 (originally published by Crown Publishers, 1985).

Woititz, Janet Geringer. *Adult Children of Alcoholics.* Hollywood, Fla.: Health Communications, 1983.

3

My Extended Family

Andrea Starr Alonzo

Obviously one of the unfortunate prerequisites to any stepfamily is divorce (or death). It is, in any case, painful for all concerned, and if the particulars of the previous relationship, either emotional or legal, are not resolved before the new party enters the picture, it's sure to complicate things even more.

When I met Brandon he was a lonely man who hung out in bars (I was working in one). As a child I was already today's modern woman and I promised myself not to marry until my late twenties. I didn't want to be a child bride; I wanted to experience life first. Then, at twenty-five, when something in me clicked and said it was time to meet Mr. Right, I met Brandon. One slight fact that I had failed to consider in my perfect plan was that at our ages (Brandon is six years older than I) we would certainly by then have a past. My own was fairly uncomplicated—no marriages, no children. Brandon, however, was a different story.

One night a couple of months after I was hooked, it occurred to me to ask how a great guy like Brandon could reach his early thirties without getting "caught." It turned out that he had, still, a wife and two daughters. In the same breath I was told that the marriage was over, and now he "had a reason to get a divorce." It didn't *sound* like a line then, and I believed it. But here I was, the "other woman." I detested the idea of being in love with a man who was legally bound to someone else even if, as he'd told me, his wife had left him. The fuzziness surrounding Brandon's relationship with his wife (now his ex-wife) and his delayed divorce turned out to be the stormiest issue in our relationship before we married.

Meanwhile, I soon met Brandon's daughters, ages five and ten, two beautiful brown-skinned dolls who had both inherited their father's large eyes. We got along just fine. They never seemed ruffled by the fact that their daddy had a girlfriend, although they had their particular ways of dealing with it. The older one, Myla, was especially protective of her mother's image. She was always careful not to reveal much about her, particularly if it was unflattering. Often I would catch her nudge her sister, Joy, who at five would indiscriminately blurt out anything that came to mind. I respected Myla's way of handling the situation. I, in turn, have always been sensitive enough not to infringe on their mother's sovereign place in their lives.

I did see the children fairly often at first, although there were always hassles about the mother letting them go. Often Brandon would drive all the way to New Jersey to pick them up and return a couple of hours later, long-faced and empty-handed. I would always be heartbroken and furious myself. Intimidated by her tactics, he went to get the girls less and less. Now I rarely see them.

Nevertheless we managed to have lots of fun times together, and as Myla approached her teen years we grew closer. She found that she could talk to me in a way that she never could with her mother. I think she enjoyed having a grown-up for a friend. Myla had a tendency toward sullenness, though, that caused problems later.

We saw how much the girls enjoyed being with their father. He said it was because they witnessed a side of him they never saw at home—a happy side. Since I'd never met the mother, I began to form my own opinions, which naturally weren't good. Especially when I heard of little incidents, such as the time Joy was writing Christmas cards and her mother caught her writing one for me—she snatched it from her and tore it up. I began to want to "rescue" them from that unhappy woman. We even talked of having them come and live with us after we were married.

Finally Brandon got his divorce, and we made immediate plans to get married. Our first son, Jason, was on the way, and we hadn't a moment to waste. I had encouraged Brandon to talk openly with his daughters about all this, and he said he would. When I asked him how they had responded to the news of our wedding, he said, "Fine." When I subsequently mentioned it to them over the phone, I got a completely different reaction. They were shocked and upset (they didn't even know!). This was the first open display of rejection they had ever shown toward me. Not an unreasonable reaction under the circumstances. They, especially Joy, had been hoping for a reconciliation between their parents.

Meanwhile, another wrinkle began to form. I was in graduate school and working odd jobs. I stopped working altogether when Jason was born. We were having money problems, and the child-support money dwindled, then stopped. While this would have made an excellent excuse for the mother, I somehow felt it was really not the basis for the limited visitation. Nevertheless, even though we were broke, I felt that Brandon should have somehow done better by the girls. Not seeing them *and* not paying? There was already a part of me that was guilty for having their father when they didn't. So no matter how broke we were, I would never deny them for us. This became an issue well into our marriage. I used to nag him like crazy to find a way to get them the money they deserved (and us, too, poor thing) and fight for his right to see them. I'd tell him that they'd grow to resent him. He seemed to believe, however, that they would grow up and see the mother as the villain in all this. I doubt it. She's got the upper hand. And she apparently does nothing to uphold their image of their father. She'd tell them that their father wasn't supporting them financially. She told Myla that we were not legally married because they were not divorced. She even pulled a stunt straight out of a soap opera: not long after our first child was born, she had a baby, and she tried to put the word out in the family that Brandon was the father. Thank God this seed of doubt didn't take root.

I guess there are any number of reasons why a man who loves his family would distance himself from them, besides dollars and cents. Not giving financial support breeds guilt and embarrassment. Or, as in Brandon's case, dealing with their mother may be an excruciating experience. Maybe he even subconsciously wants to punish her for denying him his children. The money-visitation issue is really a vicious cycle. Then too, having a part-time relationship with one's children is much more difficult than a full-time one. It's easier not to deal with painful situations; it's easier to put them off. I think the tendency for men to do this is greater than for women. When Brandon does communicate with their mother, it's usually through Joy. He avoids direct confrontation with her as much as possible. He never refers to her by her name, always as "the children's mother."

To add to things, Brandon and Myla have a strange relationship. Brandon has tended to outwardly favor Joy, who has a visibly sweeter disposition. As Myla got older, she became moodier. Even so, I could still communicate with her pretty well. As she entered her teens and began to experience discord with her mother, she'd drop complaints about her, which I'd happily lap up. The first antimaternal outburst occurred when Myla's mother made her have her hair cut when she was twelve. I was surprised at this display of anger toward her mother; from there, unfortunately it got worse.

At fifteen, Myla and I had another enlightening conversation. I was braiding her hair, which generally relaxes the tongue, and she began to explain to me her feelings about her father's marriage to me. She told me she was glad her father had married me. I couldn't believe I was hearing this.

"But what about your reaction when we told you about the wedding?" I asked her.

She explained that that was because it happened so suddenly. They hadn't had the chance to adjust to a divorce between their parents. That was a legitimate complaint, I felt. She went on to say that she realized her father was unhappy with her mother, and that she really didn't think her mom was cut out for wife- and motherhood. She was unaffectionate and insensitive. That sounded like an astute assessment of her mother from what I'd heard.

A typically rebellious teenager, Myla became increasingly difficult for all of us to cope with. They reside in an affluent town in New Jersey, and Myla of course wants to keep up with the crowd, which is wealthy kids who are often granted the freedom and money to do as they please. She refuses to understand that her parents can't afford that world. Eventually we began to hear rumors that Myla was smoking cigarettes and marijuana. She began to stay out whenever she wished, and her mother couldn't do a thing with her. Once she even called Brandon to help discipline Myla for getting caught smoking in school. Myla began to be rude to me and show open resentment toward her father. I finally had to give her my first "scolding" about respect for her father, regardless of his shortcomings. I think I did a pretty good job, because she apologized and things were all right between them for a while.

A few months ago, however, she and her father got into the last in a series of explosive fights. She was arguing with her mother when Brandon happened to be there, and he tried to intervene, whereupon Myla locked herself into the bathroom and yelled through the door at Brandon. "Go away! You're not my father! Go back to Anne and the boys. You've never been a father to me, so just get out of my life!" Brandon stopped speaking to her.

When graduation rolled around, I had to urge him to go. "You're the adult," I told him. "You can't afford to miss this milestone in her life by holding grudges. You have to set the example," He went, they kissed and made up, and we're all proud of what a fine young lady she's grown up to be. She's still sullen, though.

She had also invited me to attend the ceremonies, but I made the excuse that it was a school day, and I had to get the boys to bed. I really wanted her mother to be able to enjoy this event without any discomfort. She'd earned it. I had long since begun to soften my attitude toward her, despite her acts. A broken marriage, for whatever reasons, is a difficult thing. Yet she had, with or without the help of her husband, put one child through high school and was well on the way to putting the other. They weren't rich, but the children wanted for nothing in the way of material needs or comforts. If she's fallen short on the other part, well, who's perfect? She'd done a good job.

Brandon has been supporting them fairly regularly this year. He and Myla are speaking, and a lot of the rough edges have smoothed out. I admit that there have been times when I've wished that it was just Brandon and me, and that he didn't have such concrete reminders of his life before me. For me, the main thrust of being a stepmother is simply that they are an extension of their father, whom I love. I share some of the excitement, pride, apprehension, and pain of watching them grow. But I have never tried to force my "stepmother" status upon them, whatever that means. It wasn't until a few weeks ago, when Myla accompanied me to the hairdresser's and he asked her relationship to me, when she first heard me identify her as my stepdaughter. I deemphasize that title as much as possible. To them I am simply their father's wife.

My stormy relationship (or lack of one) with Brandon's ex-wife notwithstanding, I believe my tendency to downplay the "step" part of my family is a common trait in black culture. If you ask my Guyanese husband how many sisters and brothers he has, he'll tell you, "thirty-nine." Well, of course many of them are "steps," but they are not labeled that way. I have *never* heard my husband refer to his father's wife as his stepmother, and I seriously doubt if that term ever entered his mind. For one thing, blacks tend to feel their mothers' special place is sacred and cannot be tampered with. I once had a student who said, "As long as I have my mother, I wouldn't call anyone my stepmother."

Another cultural explanation for the lack of distinction between "steps" may lie in an old African tradition that is still prevalent in many parts of the continent: polygamous relationships. In African culture the more wives and children a man has, the wealthier he is. This precept has continued to flourish among blacks in Western civilization. What else would you call a man who has thirty-nine children by four women? And it's common knowledge among them! Of course he couldn't marry them all; it's illegal. And of course he doesn't say (or probably even recognize) that he's practicing polygamy. Technically he's not, since he's not married to them all. But no matter what we call it, this strong cultural tradition must surely have ramifications in transported Africans.

My husband made me painfully aware of this idea when I couldn't understand (was in fact quite condemning of) his mother for continuing to have children by a man she knew she'd never marry. Similarly, she's in a panic for her eldest granddaughter, nearing thirty, to begin having children before it's too late. Never mind that she can't marry the man (he's already married). To her, marriage is nice, but having children is more important.

That's why when Jason was on the way, Brandon's attitude toward marriage was "What's the rush?"

My mother's explanation for "outside" children is closely linked to the African one. She attributes it to the black man's lack of power in Western society. This is by way of justifying her own father's case. She, of course the all-time bourgeois, ignores her "halfs" as much as possible. That must be the white, middle-class thing to do. To the rest of the Jordans, however, Sam, Bud, and Edith are family. Again, though, we see the "children are wealth" principle.

"Outside" relationships and children are nothing new in any society, human beings being what they are. It's how they are treated that's different. For mainstream Americans it was always something to hide. But for blacks, the closer they are culturally to their African roots, the less of a hidden taboo it is when out-of-wedlock parenting occurs. The new wave of divorces has made the multiple family more of an issue for us all. But for blacks, stepfamilies are simply another form of the extended family.

4

Stepmother

Carol Ascher

Louise pulled a cigarette from her smooth leather purse as she and her stepdaughter inched their way out of the theater toward the crowded lobby.

"Shall we go for coffee or soda?" she asked, touching the soft skin of Ricky's arm.

Going for something to eat had become part of their theater afternoons together. For almost a year, Ricky had come in alone on the bus—a big step, at first, for a sheltered twelve-year-old girl—and the two had spent their Saturday afternoons together. When Louise and Ricky sat next to each other in the red velvet seats of a theater, they created a protected space where fondness reigned. Louise felt her mouth go dry at the thought of losing these afternoons.

"You know where I'd like to go?" Ricky asked, as she flung her arms into her woolen coat. "To the Stage Delicatessen, where we got those huge turkey sandwiches and saw Kris Kristoffersen. Remember?"

Louise smiled. "We could do that. But I'd sort of like to go someplace where I could have a drink. I think I know a restaurant you'll really love!"

Louise opened her arm so that Ricky could link hers through it, but Ricky tucked her hand in the silky lining of her stepmother's coat pocket and grinned up at her as she squeezed up against the fur coat like a cat.

All this they had together, thought Louise as she led Ricky in and out among the shoppers to 57th Street and the Russian Tea Room. The question was, could they keep it up without Donald, the husband-father who connected them?

"Stepmother" received a PEN/NEA Syndicated Short Fiction award in 1983. It was originally published in Sunday news magazines around the country and in *Arts Review*, Winter of 1987, as well as in *The Available Press: PEN Short Story Collection* (New York: Ballantine, 1985). Copyright © 1983 by Carol Ascher.

Louise had been nearly twenty-nine—a journalist who was doing well because she had given everything to her career—when she had met and rapidly married the elusive Donald. Then, what she had seen was that he would give her the time and space to continue her work. Now she looked back on five hard years of quenching Donald's first wife's anger, of finding a way to be with Ricky that everyone could tolerate, of holding Donald to her and to her home. She had had to step so carefully; and always, she had felt her hands were tied.

Louise inhaled her cigarette, drawing in the smoke to stop the dark thoughts. Ricky was wearing the camel's-hair coat she and Donald had given her for Christmas. The girl's black curly hair shone like an eclipsed sun above the collar. Ricky had a face like a Mediterranean Lolita. And just these last months, little mounds had appeared like soft marshmallows through her sweaters. Soon she would begin to go out with boys. From Louise's own selfish viewpoint, Ricky's had been a short childhood.

Everything seemed to fall through Louise's bound hands. Donald, whom she still loved with a swell of pain, when had he walked out with his suitcase? Was it two weeks or three weeks already? Somewhere another woman believed that she could hold him; but she too would become confused between an arm extended in love and in grasping, until Donald would once more be on his way.

"Did you like the play?" Ricky was asking in her sweet bouncy voice.

Louise felt the question like an offering. "I don't know. I used to like it a great deal," she said, collecting herself. "I used to think *A Doll's House* was one of the great plays. I used to love Nora's final speech when she's leaving Torvald."

Every woman dreamed of being Nora, Louise thought, a delicate flower breaking out at last from the protective love of her husband into full womanly independence. Yet it rarely happened that way. Instead, Donald had left Ricky's mother (a strong and resourceful woman like herself), just as he had now left her for another woman who would probably have much to give.

"Listen," she said, putting her arm around Ricky and giving her a squeeze, "that play is from a time when it seemed that if women could just leave men they could be whole beings. I guess it's still true." After all, she had come to understand Donald, see his grave inadequacies, without being able to leave him. "Only maybe the men get to it first," she gave a hard laugh. "I don't know, it all seems much more complicated."

"Torvald wasn't such a good husband. I didn't like him," Ricky said decisively.

"No, he's not very likeable in the end." Louise squeezed again, as if protecting Ricky from a strong wind.

They had reached the Russian Tea Room, with its darkened windows and thick, discreet door. Louise steered Ricky through the guilded entrance, and they gave their coats to the woman in the hat-check booth. An elderly waiter in a red jacket led them to a table for two along one of the mirrored walls. The Edwardian lamps and heavy silver gave the room an Old World opulence, and made it seem as if they were royalty or actors on an elegant stage. Ricky blew out her cheeks and opened her black eyes wide. Louise winked.

"Do you come here a lot?" Ricky fingered the pink damask table-cloth.

"Not a lot, but sometimes. Sometimes I come here for business lunches." Louise remembered how, as a dazzled teenager, she had first gazed at the Stork Club with the same wondrous eyes. The Club no longer existed, she didn't know when it had come down.

"It's really elegant! I bet famous people come here," Ricky said, always on the lookout.

Louise smiled. "Maybe we'll even see some."

When the waiter came, Louise ordered a double scotch and a bowl of borscht. "Why don't you try a Russian crepe?" she suggested.

"What's that?" Ricky wrinkled her nose.

"A pancake filled with sour cream and caviar."

"Will I like it?"

"I think so. Try it. You can order something else later, if you don't."

"Okay."

Louise felt her mind pulling away again. How was she to bring up the subject? Should she just start talking? Why couldn't Donald have done this before leaving town? When the scotch arrived, she gulped it down. The heat burned her throat and stomach like a shock, and for a moment her mind clouded.

Ricky had started to chatter about *The Treasure of the Sierre Madre*, which she had seen on late-night television. She was a movie fan, and sometimes stayed up till all hours by herself. "You can ask me what year it was made," she said.

"What year?" asked Louise.

"Nineteen forty-three," Ricky said, beaming. "Ask me other Bogart movies. Also who starred in them."

Louise complied, but her mind wandered. How had Ricky gotten this exaggerated energy for competence, so like Donald's? It was strange how a man could leave his family for all but rare Sunday visits, and still pieces of his personality would stay with them.

The crepe came. Ricky puffed out her cheeks at the delicate pancake, with its white cream floating outward and tiny black fish eggs like black-birds sailing over a cloud.

"We had caviar once at home, and I didn't like it," Ricky admitted. "But I think this is going to be more like a blintz."

How did one say it? How did one discuss it with a twelve-year-old? Your father and I . . . What was the end of the sentence? What questions and answers followed? For a moment, she felt almost grateful to Donald for having forced the situation. Yet why should his daughter go through this a second time?

"Is it good?" she asked, seeing Ricky's confused face.

"I think so. I can't tell yet."

"Do you want to taste my borscht?"

"In a minute." Ricky spread her pink napkin neatly on her lap.

Louise's own mother had warned her against Donald. She had said that a man running from a marriage would leave her as he had left his wife. She still had her mother to tell about Donald.

Louise smiled at Ricky spooning the thick cream. "Well, I guess the caviar's okay."

At home, what she had feared was crying like a victim as she told the girl, or, as bad, showing the anger she felt toward Donald. But now the tears she felt behind her heavy eyelids were for Ricky. A woman at work had once said how her child had kept her going in the first months after her husband had left. A mother could touch the skin of her child for hope when her courage faltered. Yet Ricky had come with, and might well leave with, the father.

Ricky was looking up at her with a serious expression. "I forgot, I wanted to ask you something."

Louise tensed. Could the girl have figured out what was happening? What traces might Donald have carelessly left?

"I've been thinking about my name. Do you think I should call myself by my real name?"

Louise's diaphragm relaxed, and the breath she took was almost pain-ful. "You mean Rebecca?"

"Mommy doesn't like the name, because she says Daddy made her name me after his mother. But I think I should use my real name. What do you think, is it a good name?"

"I like the name. Rebecca." Louise rolled out the letters slowly, aware that she was entering a web of parental bitterness. "I think Rebecca is a good name." She sipped the watery end of her scotch. "But then fashions in names change, so it's hard to say what kind of name you'll want when you're in high school or college."

"Ricky," the girl wrinkled her nose, and the dark of her nostrils twitched like a filly. "It just sounds too boyish."

"It's getting pretty hard for you to seem boyish these days," Louise teased.

"Well, I think I might start using Rebecca. Daddy will be pleased, won't he?"

"Probably." Louise smiled, and her lips seemed cracked and dry.

While Ricky went to the bathroom, Louise paid the check. They had finished eating without her being able to say anything. Perhaps out on the street, she thought, with the noise of cars and the rush of people; here everything seemed too solemn.

Outside, the street lights had come on. The greenish color of the early evening sky sent a rush of pleasure through Louise. She would be all right on her own: she'd make plans and meet new people. And she would find a way to keep Ricky in her life.

"Let's walk back to the bus depot," she said, taking Ricky's arm.

They strolled along Broadway, slowing down in front of the stores that sold cheap costume jewelry, theater makeup, and exotic undergarments. Louise remembered Ricky had once asked her if she would ever buy the brassieres with holes for the nipples. Feeling relaxed, Louise had confided, "No, but sometimes I'd like to," and they both had giggled. A little farther south were the shops selling exaggerated platform shoes, and then on 47th Street, the big Castro Convertible sofa store with its couches like giant colorful snakes filling the show windows.

"Listen," said Louise, with a sudden burst of courage. "Your father and I aren't going to live with each other any more."

She felt Ricky's body slow down deep inside, as if the machinery had hit a chink and was coming to a slow stop. There must be another sentence she ought to add, something to smooth it out and make it less abrupt.

"What I mean is, he and I probably aren't going to be married any longer. I think your father feels he's been married basically all his adult life, since he was very young. You know, he married your mother and then right away he married me." How reasonable it sounded; of course he would want to leave.

"You mean, you're going to get a divorce?"

Louise searched for a cigarette in her leather purse. She lit one and drew in a long breath. "Yes, probably, but not right away. What we're going to do now is live separately. He'll probably be able to tell you more when you see each other, but I wanted to tell you myself." Perhaps it wasn't her right to tell Ricky, but Donald had left town without telling his daughter— the one piece of his behavior that could infuriate her whenever she recalled it. With his busy schedule, his traveling, and his reluctance to confront difficult matters, Louise knew it would be months before he told his daughter. He would even be pleased that she had said something, relieved him of that awful first sentence she herself had found so hard. "I don't know; maybe he should have told you first."

"No, that's good," Ricky answered distractedly. She was working out something in her mind. Finally she said, "Does that mean you won't be my stepmother any more?"

"Did you think of me as your stepmother?" Louise answered, grateful. She had always been afraid that, with Ricky's mother taking care of the child, "stepmother" gave her more legitimacy than she was allowed.

"Sort of. A little bit. I sometimes told the kids at school I had a mother and a stepmother."

They walked awhile in silence. Louise was trying to figure out how to say that she still wanted to be Ricky's . . . But that was the problem, there would no longer be a word. Without the connection of kinship, a relationship between a grown woman and a little girl sounded pathetic and almost perverse. It made her seem too needy, like the lonely old people who had "little brothers" or played foster parents on the weekend.

"I guess we could still go to plays," she heard Ricky say, "I mean, you usually get the tickets free anyway."

That was it—how simple! "I'd take you even if I have to pay for the tickets," Louise laughed with relief.

"It's just that my mother's going to think it's really weird."

Louise felt stung. "You mean, us going to the theater together?"

"No, I mean Daddy breaking up with you."

She laughed. "I guess she'll think it serves me right."

"She didn't think Daddy should marry someone else right away."

So many complications for a girl to figure out, Louise thought. She couldn't imagine working out all these angles when she was twelve. But then even suburban girls like Ricky were more sophisticated nowadays. "Your mom was probably right," she said, offering a gesture of reconciliation toward the woman who had been such a constant shadow.

They had walked up 41st Street to avoid the wild hustle of the movies and arcades on 42nd. Now the Port of New York Authority faced them squarely, its purple brick shining new and elegant from the street lamps. Inside the Saturday night crowd was like a waterfall flowing in from one door and pouring out toward the multitude of bus outlets.

"Can I have some candy for the way home?" Ricky asked.

They stopped at a newsstand, and Louise glanced at the headlines while Ricky picked up a bag of Red Hots.

It was easy not to say anything as they moved rapidly along with the crowd through the vast depot. Louise felt the numbness of someone walking mechanically toward a fate long ago sealed.

At stall number 237, the red and tan New Jersey bus prepared to leave. Ricky stood on her toes to give a quick kiss.

Louise put her arms around the girl and held her with unexpected desperation. "Go! I love you," she said, her voice breaking.

5

benjamin

Deborah Rosenfelt

I wrote this poem when Ben's father and I had ended our relationship and I thought I would never see either of them again. Happily, I was wrong. Even after his father's subsequent death, Ben's mother, newly remarried and living in another state, encouraged the two of us to keep in touch. Now Ben visits me sometimes—and plays big brother to the daughter I adopted when I realized, through him, how much I wanted to mother and how deeply I could love a child "not of my body."

Child not of my body
You come to me in my dreams

No labor of mine impelled you into life
I felt no awe
When your first words rose like dumplings

When you explored the empty air
By the third-floor window
No terror urged me gasping through the night
Ignorantly I moved
Down other streets
In another city

I knew what would be
                    for the father
The rage in   the ache for   the flesh
    the lean and lank and bone of him
    the sweet gold bud of his lust.

Who could have—
How can I—
Child not of my body—
Foretold, appease
This other hunger?

You dance for me in my dreams
Child not of my body
You swim to sleep in my arms
You ride the difficult alleys
Never using your hands

You call to me in my dreams
Child not of my flesh
You call to me from doorways
From the secret banks of streams.

I answer.
I wake.

In a year you'll forget my face
In two, my name

There is no name for this loss.

Child not of my blood
I could build your bones from the dust.

6

Parenting on the Edge

Sophia Carestia

Being on the edge is paradoxical. Sometimes I'm on the sidelines, left out, "on the fringe." Other times I think I'm on the edge of a wonderful discovery, on the cutting edge, in the vanguard, handling an extended family in a new and better way. Until I find myself torn between good intentions and the pull of circumstances; then the cutting edge is on me, a razor to my heart. But it is certainly an interesting vantage point and, yes, the view from the edge can be exhilarating if you're not too distracted watching your step.

About ten years ago, I began seeing a man recently separated from his wife and daughter. Joseph and I met while in graduate school. He still clung to his wedding band like a tiny life preserver and in those early days talked a lot about his terrific relationship with his wife, Monica.

They'd married very young, in 1969, gone to college and then graduate school together. They were very radical, extremely hip, the most hip group of people I had ever met, even though at first I could only imagine Monica and Constance. Connie, the daughter, was seven then and called her parents by their names, although, I was told, she went through about two weeks of calling them "Mom" and "Dad." The question of stepparenting hardly arises in a context where parenting itself proceeds against the institutionalized grain. I never thought of myself as any sort of parent. "Friend" was as far as I thought I could, or should, go.

Married in the late 1960s, divorced in the mid-1970s, and founding households in the 1980s. Alas, our collective experience seemed to mirror the decades in true *People* magazine style. First rebellion, heady and sweet. Then retrenchment and a search for our selves, all four of us. The mean

1980s found Connie grown up to be a gorgeous suburban shoe fetishist in the Sunbelt with Monica, who had established a great pair of careers but not found a permanent partner. Joseph and I worked like crazy in New York and wished we could afford a down payment on anything that didn't have a landlord attached.

The idealism all of us share is not something any of us will give up. We three adults are all left-leaning academics and writers. Connie, for all of her teenage *sang-froid,* does write letters to the editor and counsel other teens on drug abuse. We have enjoyed being critical, nonviolent intellectuals, devoted to an egalitarian ethic of nonconfrontation. But in many ways these ideals backfired on us as we tried to live through the past decade. Perhaps our solutions were too creative.

Take the matter of getting to know one another. At first, Monica wanted to meet me; she thought I sounded "good" for Joseph. We were all so civilized, so laid back, and so unanxious about all this, wouldn't it be nice? Luckily, geography intervened, and we put off getting acquainted for six years. Yes, you've noticed the first peculiarity here, right?

We always seemed to have good intentions. We just had difficulty carrying them out. It began with the divorce itself eight years ago, when the promised agreement on joint custody didn't quite work out. Monica's lawyer simply stood up and filed for sole custody, surprising the hell out of Joseph, who hadn't even retained a lawyer.

And then all our visits together with Connie. She would stay three or four times a year, holidays and summer vacations. We'd all try to plan, with great good will, the when, how, and what. Connie would spend hours on the phone with her father. He'd say, Well why don't you and Monica make the reservations convenient to you? And she'd say, Great. Monica would get on the phone. He'd say, How about those reservations? She'd say, Great. I'd say (after they hung up), Maybe we ought to do it. No, everything was just fine. Next week we'd go through it all again until finally someone would grab the last seat on the most expensive flight between Tampa and New York. And believe me, we all *wanted* to see each other.

This particular example of our team's disorganization culminated one Christmas. Monica and Connie were in the Northeast with grandparents and Joseph was anxious (he was sitting up by late 1985, a little less laid back) to spend a week with Connie. Various family problems intervened and Connie's one-hour plane ride was put off again and again. By the time she arrived at 8:00 P.M. on New Year's Eve, Joseph was standing up, ready to kill. So how did we pass the evening?

Very pleasantly, of course. Because her father is not part of her everyday life, Connie cannot bear any conflict with him or about him. That night, no one said anything to anyone about how tough the past week had been. (She was fifteen by then; were the snafus in plans, the endless delays and dillydallying still the fault of her mother?) Connie, caught in the middle, preserved a discreet silence. She admired my hair, I admired her boots, she borrowed my jacket. And the whole gang trooped off to Danceteria to disco the night away.

Last Christmas we did considerably better. For one thing, Joseph and I announced our "engagement." Yes, after knowing each other for ten years and sharing a household for five, we decided to marry. Our parents got together for dinner. Joseph told Monica, who was thunderstruck. He told Connie, who sweetly congratulated him. (She and I have yet to discuss it.)

We can't help but notice, however, that since the announcement, Monica carefully includes me much more in plans and conversations. I suddenly feel obliged to inquire more closely into her life. Things have changed. This is not to say our commitment to alternative lifestyles was wasted or even gone. But it does point up how the sum of the gazes of others combines with economic necessity (can we call this "society"?) to weigh upon even the most fervent personal dedication. (Should we have married sooner? Would it have made a difference? It seems to have.)

Which brings me to our central anecdote. Connie very much wanted her father to attend her high school commencement in Tampa. She also invited me. Now although Connie has often invited Joseph to visit her in Florida, he has never managed to get there. Mostly because it was the scene of the breakup of his marriage and he had ugly memories of a good thing gone bad. But also because every time he brought it up, Monica would insist that he could stay at their house. Clearly this was not what Joseph had in mind. (What are the limits to the friendship that a former spouse can insist upon "for the sake of the children"?) Half included in these double-binding and loaded invitations (Joseph invited me, just adding to his problems), I certainly hadn't pushed for immediately getting on a plane.

During Connie's Easter vacation, we planned excitedly the trip to Florida. She'd drive us around in her vintage Mustang, or lend it to us. We'd have hours at the beach. She and her dad would show me all the best places for seafood. Her friends would meet her youthful-looking father; she was very proud of his looks. She left New York, promising to find us an inexpensive, quaintly tacky, and not too high-tech motel on the beach.

I started hearing Joseph on the phone saying, So how about that hotel? Oh, no time yet; well, OK, but listen, honey, we need to make plane reservations. After three Sunday evenings of this, I finally marched to the travel agent to buy a package deal. I did have the sense, however, to call Connie and ask if the Green Flamingo was okay. (How horrible if I were to be responsible for depositing her father in an "uncool" place.)

She was surprised to hear from me, and I felt a little sad. There was a pause as I mentioned the Green Flamingo. It was okay, she thought it was funny, they'd just had a party there last week. I was worried. I wondered about the hotel; I wondered about Connie's parties. (There had been a time, when she was fourteen or fifteen, that she confided in me about the teenage wasteland of Tampa. Alas, this had stopped in the last two years). I wondered if Connie would ever, in fact, say, "It's an awful roach dump, a super massage parlor." No, I decided, she wouldn't. She was too discreet to incriminate herself and disappoint me.

It was set. We started to work on our tans in the back yard. (I bought SPF 8 sunscreen anyway.) Then, three days before we were to leave, Monica called. (Now remember, all this comes secondhand from Joseph, who works very hard making everyone sound good to everyone else.) It seems that the social leader of Connie's class had parents who were planning a champagne reception before commencement. But only "real" parents were invited; each kid could bring only two. (One of each sex, one presumes. It was the Stern-Whitehead approach to parenting: only those who had contributed genetic matter could come—to hell with nurture, this was a celebration of nature. Perhaps they'd pass out little "egg" and "sperm" buttons. If I could smuggle myself in would that make me a "stepegg"?)

Monica said that Connie was embarrassed and didn't want to bring it up because of me. Joseph was angry and said, Connie was right, it shouldn't have been brought up at all. Why are you bringing it up? I couldn't go, he wouldn't go, and she shouldn't go. Of course, of course, Monica hastened to agree. It was a terribly stupid and reactionary idea. Well, bye, see you Wednesday.

I guess I had a low moment in my years of "nonstepparenting" when he told me about this conversation (one of hundreds of "My Conversations with Monica" I have listened to over the years). I ranted. I raved. I struck theatrical poses. Right. No gigolos, no floozies, no new husbands, no second wives allowed. My distress at being summarily dealt out of "parenting" surprised me; was I more interested in the role than I thought? I forlornly contemplated my new floral beach shorts. Not even my new status as "fiancee" could help me now; I was in for it.

We arrived blinking and sweating in the Florida sun. No Connie to meet the plane. Then, in one of those fits of parental insight that almost do make you believe in the magic of "genetic matter," Joseph went off to find her at the baggage carousel. She looked wonderful—tanned, blonde, and genuinely happy. After an embarrassing moment when we thought the Mustang was lost, Connie whizzed us off to her house.

It was great to see her room, her cats, her prom photos. Even the trees outside had been described in detail. It didn't matter that we felt a bit awkward standing around in the clean kitchen, listening to the air conditioning hum. We invited her to dinner, but Connie had to pick up her friend Cheryl, who was flying in for graduation weekend. So Joseph and I took off for the hotel, leaving her to wait for her mother's car to come home with her mother from work.

The coming of Cheryl did not please Joseph. The next day, she and Connie arrived at the beach, promptly swam for half an hour, then went up to our room to "dry off," only to come down and announce they were going for some lunch. Joseph wondered aloud if Cheryl would tag along all weekend. As it turned out, it didn't much matter. Connie was so busy, we barely saw her. Of course, it was graduation; there were parties and then the mornings after parties.

In fact, it became painfully obvious that, after all those years, when she finally had her father there in Florida, Connie didn't know what to do with him. One afternoon, in desperation, we stopped in after looking around Tampa. Connie stood at the door chatting with Joseph, who'd run to see if she was home. She didn't invite him in. He stood in the 97-degree heat, I sat in the 98-percent humidity in the car, and Connie unconsciously guarded her, and her mother's, air-conditioned sanctum. (We knew her boyfriend was working, so it wasn't that.)

It was even worse for Monica, who tried to make us both welcome. Perhaps a buffet before commencement with all of *her* friends, some of whom had been water carriers during the divorce, wasn't the best way to do that. Nonetheless, in our usual fashion we all tried to rise above petty feelings of regret, jealousy, and anxiety. (Joseph regretted not seeing more of Connie, Monica was jealous seeing us up close, and I was anxious about everything.) But face to face this was much harder.

What did we expect, turning up on their territory after all these years? That territory was far from New York City. Connie grew up in a nice, clean suburb, in a world where leisure time was considered an opportunity to shop. For some reason, it was thought that parental models of serious reading and serious politics would outweigh the material facts of the local mall as social center. Of course, that was not so.

And then, speaking personally, Connie couldn't foresee that in fact, once we set foot in their house, she would adopt her mother's attitudes of distanced politeness. Monica's dogged ability to remain cool under fire seemed to put a damper on us all. We stood around in the heat, pretending to be cool as cucumbers, saying far less than we could on the phone.

Joseph thinks Connie was completely boggled by having to deal with both her parents at the same time, and "at home" for the first time since the divorce. Unwilling to play favorites, she reacted with utter fairness and ignored both of them—and all nearby adults. Cool detachment had, after all, been a style presented to Connie since she'd been very small.

If Joseph is right, should we opt for passion, have a "discussion," "get it all out in the open"? We don't think so. Even though we are not happy with where nonconfrontation has taken us, Joseph and Monica think that taking up any issues now may be misunderstood by Connie as claims for attention.

It is hard for divorced families to judge how much of their teenagers' behavior is reaction to the stress of separation and how much to the stress of growing up itself. Parents accustomed to providing a secure center for their young children tend to imagine that the world still revolves around them. We're trying to act as though Connie's world is now much bigger than that: it includes, especially, college in the fall and the enticing first departure from her room, her cats, and her mother's house. (Are we still kidding ourselves?)

It is harder for Monica, who has had custody of Connie and lived with her every day of her seventeen years. It is easier for Connie and Joseph, who developed ways to cope with separation long ago. For me, it will be a relief not to have Connie's contact with us mediated through Monica's relationship (or the memory of her relationship) with Joseph.

But I do know that a woman's mother is with her forever, and there is nothing that can change the fact of a history the three of them share. I have also realized, however, that because of my love for Joseph, I am thoroughly implicated in Connie's life. Being married really does matter less than shared time and experience (the real stuff of "history"). We have all, especially me, finally admitted that I helped to fashion some of the last decade of our collective past.

After graduation, we were standing in the stadium. The night was cooling down; a breeze mussed Connie's beautiful curls and she was surreptitiously trying to batten them down as her father snapped pictures. I took the camera and suggested the three of them stand together. I may not exactly be in that picture, but I helped to make it.

7

The Barbie Doll Fight

Gale McGovern

"But she has no feet."

"Sure she does. They're just not big like yours."

And that was how this particular fight had started.

Sally and Maggie were enjoying the luxury of breakfast and the Sunday papers in bed—the same bed, without the artifice of separate rooms in the same house. This was Julie's weekend with her father and his new wife, so for two days in a row Sally and Maggie could wake up together and have their morning snuggle immediately.

On weekdays they had to wait until one of them had gotten up, dressed herself and Julie, fed Julie breakfast, measured out the day's medicine, taken her to the babysitter, and come back to undress and join the other in bed, full of acrid day-energy instead of sweet-smelling sleep. The ritual of the morning snuggle in bed was so important to them that they were willing to add an extra half hour to their schedule to accommodate it.

They took turns getting Julie to the babysitter, but still there was nothing like opening your eyes and drowsily kissing your lover awake.

Maggie hated this skulking around; it was against her nature. From the first stirrings of the gay movement in the late 1960s until three years ago, when she had met Sally at a crafts show in New York City, she was out to everybody, including her boss, her co-workers, and her family. Some members of her family hadn't liked it—one brother was still not speaking to her—but when you got right down to it there was nothing they could do beyond withdrawal of affection. All in all, Maggie always said it was worth it not to have to lie or hesitate before telling the truth.

Now she lived in a small upstate town, still in culture shock from leaving Greenwich Village, and spent considerable energy propping up a lie before all but a few close friends. Maggie and Sally told people they were cousins; they kept all suspicious books and periodicals in a box in the closet; and when Julie, who was now four, began to speak in more than nouns they moved to separate bedrooms and became strict with themselves about displaying anything but the most innocent affection in front of her. All this on the advice of a feminist lawyer in New York City who specialized in lesbian custody cases.

"Supposing Julie's spending a weekend with her father," this lawyer had explained. "You say he's already told you he'd like custody but he knows he hasn't got a chance of getting her away from her mother. What if he starts pumping her for information about other men you might bring home—"

"But I never bring men home," Sally had interrupted. "I live with Maggie. We're monogamous." As if that solved all problems.

"—and Julie, in all innocence, says, 'Mommy never kisses men, Daddy, she just kisses Maggie.' "

Sally, who had never been involved with a woman before and who had not given much thought to the ways of homophobia (in fact, Maggie was the first lesbian she'd ever known up close), could not believe Jim would use that against her. And even if he did, the courts would never be so unjust as to take away her child simply because she loved another woman.

But Maggie knew better and, since she was as much in love with Julie as with Sally, said to the lawyer: "Okay. Suppose we sleep in separate bedrooms. What else?"

The lawyer suggested that they keep a log of all interactions between them and Jim, with particular attention to his failures of responsibility. She asked if they could move to a larger, more heterogeneous community, where the judges were more likely to be open-minded. But Sally's parents were here, and her pottery shop, and Jim lived in the next town, and he had been granted the right to take Julie on alternate weekends, and even now he was always complaining about the half-hour distance between them. And he had refused to even consider four days once a month. Besides, Julie was usually a wreck when she came back from two days with him: who knew what four days would do?

So here they were in bed arguing about the Barbie doll when they should have been making love.

"The issue under discussion," said Maggie, "is the Barbie doll's feet—not mine."

"All right," said Sally, "I'm sorry I put down your feet. You know I love them." She smiled coquettishly in a way that annoyed Maggie almost beyond self-containment, and tweaked Maggie's big toe.

Maggie withdrew her foot. "I'd like to discuss this seriously," she said.

Sally sat up straight. The flirtatious smile was replaced briefly by a petulant look that Maggie had almost trained her out of. At last Sally gave up her manipulative repertoire and became serious. "Okay," she said. "The question is, does Julie get to keep the Barbie doll her daddy gave her for her birthday or do I take it away from her? And if I take it away, how do I explain to a four-year-old child that her Barbie doll is politically incorrect?"

"I think that can be handled," said Maggie. "I think the question that's really bothering you is how to explain to a thirty-five-year-old Middle American man that you don't want his daughter to grow up looking like his new wife."

"What have you got against Linda? *I'm* the one who's supposed to hate her. You're supposed to be relieved that she's got the competition diverted."

"First of all, I wasn't aware that he was still the competition. You told me three years ago that you were finished with him."

"Oh, all right. I just said that to make you jealous."

"I also thought we had agreed to cut the games."

"You're right," said Sally. "I'm sorry."

"And second of all, I don't hate Linda. I hate what she represents: blond, blue-eyed, life-sized Barbie dolls who spend their whole lives trying to make some alcoholic ex-football player mow the lawn and fix the sink—"

"All right. You're starting to rant and rave again."

"Damn it. Why is it ranting and raving when I talk about feminist issues?"

"It's not that, but why can't you just lighten up? Why does it always have to be so heavy?"

"Because it's important. It matters to me. Why doesn't it matter to you? It's your daughter we're talking about."

Sally was getting bored. "Since you make that point," she said, escalating to make it more interesting, and perhaps to deflect them from the subject, "maybe you should consider what it means."

Maggie gave her an exasperated look. "Are you going to tell me it's your daughter, why don't I mind my own business? Because if you are, there are a few things maybe *you* should consider. Like whether you want to make this a power struggle over the ownership of another human being— a power struggle that you will win hands down because you have the law and society to back it up—or whether you want to retain your integrity and make this a good-faith discussion between two people who love Julie."

Sally shrugged. "Okay, you're right." They had settled that question early on, and although she still felt Julie was much more hers than theirs, she had agreed that Maggie had major rights. She tried to give her all the rights she would have given a second husband. Maggie loved Julie, she did half the childcare, she paid half the bills, she sat up all the nights when Julie was having asthma attacks. In almost every way Maggie was another mother, and yet it was not possible for Sally to think of her completely as the other parent. If Maggie were a man it might be easier: a stepfather wouldn't be challenging her own unique position as Julie's mother.

But she would never admit that to Maggie: it would hurt her too much and undermine the equality they were working so hard for. Besides, it wasn't necessary to emphasize it. The fact that she was a real mother could never be denied or taken away from her.

"Sometimes I think you resent my relationship with Julie," said Maggie.

Sally took her hand. "Not resent. I think it's beautiful. Sometimes I might get a little jealous."

Maggie knew this to be true. She was mollified.

"Let's get back to the Barbie doll," she said, shifting her body slightly so that her elbow, on which she was leaning, was on Sally's side of the imaginary line that bisected the bed. "The reason I think it's bad for Julie is the role model it sets up. The doll has no feet: that discourages independence. The breasts are pushed up: they're only for sexual purposes. The feet are extended so she's standing on tiptoe, so the only shoes you can put on her are shoes no woman could use to run away from a rapist . . ."

Sally listened as Maggie launched the Speech, maintaining an expression of respectful attention, while she thought about exactly how she would make love to this intense, passionate feminist as soon as Maggie believed she had convinced Sally to ban the Barbie doll.